THE CAPTAIN, JUNE 4, 2008

JULIAN H. GONZALEZ

THE 'FOREVER HOCKEYTOWN' BENCH

EDITOR
Mark Francescutti

DESIGN EDITOR
Ryan Ford

DESIGNERS
Ryan Ford,
Tim Good,
Jason Karas,
Jeff Tarsha

PHOTO EDITORS
Diane Weiss,
Craig Porter

PHOTO IMAGING
Rose Ann McKean

COPY EDITORS
Tim Marcinkoski,
Bill Collison,
David Darby,
Mari delaGarza,
James Jahnke,
Mary Masson,
Matt Fiorito,
Jim Dwight,
Kevin Bull,
Steve Schrader,
Kirkland Crawford

COVER PHOTO
Romain Blanquart

CONTRIBUTING WRITERS
Nick Meyer,
Eric Habermas,
Matt Cammarata,
Scott Bell

SPORTS EDITOR
Gene Myers

**PROJECT COORDINATOR,
A.M.E./PRESENTATION**
Steve Dorsey

SPECIAL THANKS
Laurie Delves,
A.J. Hartley,
Dave Robinson
and our friends at
The Anchor.

3	8	20
THE CUP	THE ROAD	THE TEAM
70	96	123
THE PLAYOFFS	THE FINALS	OCTO GARDEN

RICK NEASE

FOUR THE AGES
From Larry Aurie to Gordie Howe to Steve Yzerman, the Wings' stockpiles of Hall of Fame talent have often resulted in Stanley Cups. In 2008, it was Nicklas Lidstrom's turn to carry the torch – and the Cup.

Detroit Free Press

615 W. Lafayette Blvd..
Detroit, MI 48226
©2008 by Detroit Free Press. All rights reserved.
Manufactured by Quebecor World Dubuque, USA

OTHER RECENT FREE PRESS SPORTS BOOKS

- The Captain
- Not Till the Fat Lady Sings
- Men at Work
- Razor Sharp
- Fishing Michigan
- Hockey Gods
- Hang 10
- Believe
- Stanleytown
- Ernie Harwell: Life After Baseball
- Ernie Harwell: Stories from My Life in Baseball
- Corner to Copa
- Century of Champions
- The Corner
- State of Glory
- Roar Restored
- Long Run
- Breaking 90

 To order any of these titles or other gear, go to www.freep.com/bookstore or call 800-245-5082.

REIGN MAKERS

NEW CROWN FOR WINGS IN SAME OLD KINGDOM

BY MITCH ALBOM

One last bullet came flying at Chris Osgood. It had kill all over it. He stopped it with his glove, pushed it away with his stick, and as the blue light swirled to mark the end of the game, he was flat on the ice. The Red Wings were coming home. The Stanley Cup was coming with them. As they say in fairy tales, "All's Well That Ends Red."

Well, in Detroit fairy tales.

After six games. After six years. The Wings, knocked down in a gutting triple-overtime loss two days earlier, shook loose every demon that might have followed them to Pittsburgh and played the game they had to play.

They took a lead, and this time they held off the furious charge and a last-minute goal, enduring a final shot by Sidney Crosby that Osgood stopped with his glove and pushed far enough away to avoid a last-instant miracle by Marian Hossa.

THE WIZARD OF OZ

"It's awesome ... you can't describe it," Nicklas Lidstrom told NBC after the 3-2 victory in Game 6. "It's a great feeling."

And it's a whole new crown in the same old kingdom, Hockeytown, thanks to an unflappable band of brothers who epitomize the old and young, the foreign and North American, the cast-offs and superstars.

Here was Osgood, out of Peace River, Alberta, out of the Red Wings' past, and out of the shadows, refusing to sink to people's fears or doubts, standing tall when he had to and low when he needed to.

"I've got a bigger heart than people think," Osgood told the TV cameras.

STARTING OFF WITH A BANG

"Nicklas Lidstrom, come get the Stanley Cup," NHL commissioner Gary Bettman announced. "It's yours to take back to Hockeytown."

Lidstrom, the captain, held up the chalice, smiled broadly, then shook it at his gathered teammates who cheered like excited schoolchildren.

ROMAIN BLANQUART

FOURTH WAS A GRIND
Red Wings center and Grind Liner Kris Draper hoists and kisses the Stanley Cup for the fourth time in his career in Detroit. Draper, who has played in five Stanley Cup finals, also won the Cup in 1997, 1998 and 2002. He had three goals and one assist in this season's playoffs.

After a brief skate, he handed it not to the biggest star on the team, but to Dallas Drake, who, at 39, nearly retired before this season, having never been to a finals. And here he was, skating with the Stanley Cup.

The Wings won every playoff round on the road. And you might say the home loss that preceded the final victory was instrumental in their story. For all the impressive things Detroit had done, coming back from Game 5 has to rank high.

Men in their 30s. Younger men in their 20s. It's the Wings' best asset, a combination of youth and experience, and they employed it beautifully.

CHAMPIONS LANDING

KATHLEEN GALLIGAN

The Wings were welcomed home heroes after their fourth Stanley Cup title in 11 seasons. The party started at 2:52 a.m., shortly after the Red Wings landed at the Metro Airport's ASIG terminal. It was catered for 400 people. Most of them were drinking out of the Stanley Cup. They all celebrated as Detroit moved into third place all time in NHL titles, trailing fellow Original Six clubs Montreal and Toronto.

THE BRIGHTEST OF FUTURES

The Wings may have won this thing in six games, but let's be honest: The Penguins are a formidable young group. This 2008 version is the first modern-era Wings championship that didn't feature Steve Yzerman as captain or Scotty Bowman as coach. The first without the benefit of signing any expensive free agent.

A whole new Cup in the same old kingdom. The salary cap was supposed to be the end of Detroit dominance, but Ken Holland and Jim Nill have managed to find diamonds despite the rough, and the Wings have been a winning but uncrowned franchise since 2002.

How great was this for Babcock, who came within a hair of a Stanley Cup in Anaheim?

HAIL TO THE CAPTAIN

How great is this for Lidstrom, 38 — the first European captain on a Cup champion?

How great is this for Mike Ilitch, who continues to pour money and staff into this organization, which continues to be the envy of the NHL? He gets a title here with his original sports franchise, and nobody will be able to say he did it by emptying a bigger bank vault than his competitors. It's a salary-cap era. Everyone gets the same chips.

It's a whole new Cup in the same old kingdom. And even if it seemingly took forever, it feels right on time.

SOMETHING TO SHARE

Pavel Datsyuk celebrates the Red Wings' 11th Stanley Cup championship with Kirk Maltby. It's the second Cup for Datsyuk and the fourth for Maltby. Datsyuk scored 10 goals and 23 points in 22 playoff games. "There was a lot of talk, (Sidney) Crosby and (Evgeni) Malkin ... those guys are great hockey players, and this city (Pittsburgh), this organization has a great future," Kris Draper said. "But you know what? (Henrik) Zetterberg and Datsyuk, they made a statement this playoff run."

ROMAIN BLANQUART

CUP RUNNETH OVER
Kris Draper, left, sprays the Stanley Cup and Dallas Drake gives it a tip as goaltender Chris Osgood drinks from the NHL's Holy Grail for the third time in his career. Ozzie also won Cups in 1997 and 1998. It's Draper's fourth Cup, Drake's first.

CHAPTER TWO

THE ROAD

In their final game of the 2007 season, Game 6 of the Western Conference finals against Anaheim, Pavel Datsyuk and Henrik Zetterberg combined for three goals and one assist, pushing the Red Wings tantalizingly close to victory.

Their performances in the playoffs established just how they have become the team's leaders. They've finally learned how to arrive for playoff hockey.

All the criticisms that have been lobbed at the Wings for years — they're too old, too small, too European — linger, but the simple facts are these: The Wings can still roll four lines, start a backup goaltender who has led a team to the Stanley Cup and field a defense in possession of eight Norris trophies.

The Wings cruised to the league's best record again — 30-8-3 in the first half and 54-21-7 overall.

Here's how they did it.

STOPPERS

Dominik Hasek helped stop Anaheim's Corey Perry for a 3-2 win in the first game of the season. The Wings allowed an NHL-low 184 goals all season (2.24 per game).

JULIAN H. GONZALEZ

MOVING DAZE

Key moves in the off-season before the Wings won the Cup:

DEPARTURES

MATHIEU SCHNEIDER, ROBERT LANG AND TODD BERTUZZI
Schneider, a top defenseman, lives in Manhattan Beach, Calif., so he signed with Anaheim. Lang (signed with Chicago) was a disappointment in 2007's playoffs and had a poor relationship with coach Mike Babcock. Forward Bertuzzi (signed with Anaheim) never was 100% healthy with the Wings.

ARRIVALS

BRIAN RAFALSKI, DALLAS DRAKE
GM Ken Holland plucked Rafalski, who grew up in Dearborn, about an hour after losing Schneider to the Ducks. The Wings added depth by signing ex-Wing Drake to a one-year deal. Drake's agitating style fit on the third or fourth line.

REUNIONS

DOMINIK HASEK, CHRIS CHELIOS
The Wings brought back two veterans for less than $3 million total.

FOR OPENERS

STARTING LINEUP
The Wings opened the season with minds on improving upon their 2007 finish in the Western Conference finals. "Knowing what it's like in the playoffs, going through a grueling series like we did, really, all three series, it just helps to have gone through something like that," Nicklas Lidstrom said.

JULIAN H. GONZALEZ

FREE PRESS PREDICTIONS

MICHAEL ROSENBERG
WINGS' FINISH: Conf. finals.
STANLEY CUP: Rangers over Ducks.

DREW SHARP
WINGS' FINISH: Conf. finals.
STANLEY CUP: Rangers over Ducks.

HELENE ST. JAMES
WINGS' FINISH: Cup win.
STANLEY CUP: Wings over Penguins.

GEORGE SIPPLE
WINGS' FINISH: Cup finals.
STANLEY CUP: Rangers over Wings.

A LOOK BACK AT THE WINGS BEFORE THE SEASON BEGAN

HOW THEY ARRIVED IN HOCKEYTOWN

Breaking down each Wing's path to Detroit

NO	POS	NAME	ACQUIRED
8	LW	JUSTIN ABDELKADER	Drafted by Wings in 2005 (Round 2, No. 42 overall).
24	D	CHRIS CHELIOS	Acquired from Chicago in trade, March 23, 1999.
11	RW	DAN CLEARY	Signed as free agent, Oct. 4, 2005.
13	C	PAVEL DATSYUK	Drafted by Wings in 1998 (Round 6, No. 171 overall).
20	RW	AARON DOWNEY	Signed as free agent, Oct. 3, 2007.
17	RW	DALLAS DRAKE	Signed as free agent, July 9, 2007.
33	C	KRIS DRAPER	Acquired from Winnipeg in trade, June 30, 1993.
52	D	JONATHAN ERICSSON	Drafted by Wings in 2002 (Round 9, No. 291 overall).
51	C	VALTTERI FILPPULA	Drafted by Wings in 2002 (Round 3, No. 95 overall).
93	C	JOHAN FRANZEN	Drafted by Wings in 2004 (Round 3, No. 97 overall).
44	C	MARK HARTIGAN	Signed as free agent, July 16, 2007.
39	G	DOMINIK HASEK	Signed as free agent, July 31, 2006.
43	C	DARREN HELM	Drafted by Wings in 2005 (Round 5, No. 132 overall).
96	LW	TOMAS HOLMSTROM	Drafted by Wings in 1994 (Round 10, No. 257 overall).
35	G	JIMMY HOWARD	Drafted by Wings in 2003 (Round 2, No. 64 overall).
26	C	JIRI HUDLER	Drafted by Wings in 2002 (Round 2, No. 58 overall).
82	RW	TOMAS KOPECKY	Drafted by Wings in 2000 (Round 2, No. 38 overall).
55	D	NIKLAS KRONWALL	Drafted by Wings in 2000 (Round 1, No. 29 overall).
22	D	BRETT LEBDA	Signed as free agent, July 21, 2004.
5	D	NICKLAS LIDSTROM	Drafted by Wings in 1989 (Round 3, No. 53 overall).
3	D	ANDREAS LILJA	Signed as free agent, Aug. 24, 2005.
18	LW	KIRK MALTBY	Acquired from Edmonton in trade, March 20, 1996.
25	RW	DARREN MCCARTY	Signed as free agent, Feb. 25, 2008.
14	D	DEREK MEECH	Drafted by Wings in 2002 (Round 7, No. 229 overall).
30	G	CHRIS OSGOOD	Signed as free agent, Aug. 8, 2005.
45	D	KYLE QUINCEY	Drafted by Wings in 2003 (Round 4, No. 132 overall).
28	D	BRIAN RAFALSKI	Signed as free agent, July 1, 2007.
42	C	MATTIAS RITOLA	Drafted by Wings in 2005 (Round 4, No. 103 overall).
37	RW	MIKAEL SAMUELSSON	Signed as free agent, Sept. 17, 2005.
36	D	GARRETT STAFFORD	Signed as free agent, July 16, 2007.
23	D	BRAD STUART	Acquired from Los Angeles in trade, Feb. 26, 2008.
40	LW	HENRIK ZETTERBERG	Drafted by Wings in 1999 (Round 7, No. 210 overall).

NATIONAL PREDICTIONS

BARRY MELROSE, ESPN

"Are they good enough to take a run at San Jose or Anaheim in the West? I'm not sure about that. "

E.J. HRADEK, ESPN

"They won't be quite as good."

THE OTHERS

KEVIN ALLEN, USA TODAY: Penguins over Ducks.

MIKE BREHM, USA TODAY: Wings over Penguins.

DAN FRIEDELL, USA TODAY.COM: Penguins over Wings.

JOHN GLENNON, THE TENNESSEAN: Sharks over Senators.

DARREN ELIOT, VERSUS: Senators over Sharks.

THE SEASON
SEASON IN REVIEW

FAST-FORWARD!

BIG GOALS! BIG DEALS! BIG WINS! CATCH UP WITH THE WINGS' RUN THROUGH THE REGULAR SEASON

BY GEORGE SIPPLE

HOCKEYTOWN?

OCT. 3: The Red Wings opened the season with a 3-2 shoot-out victory over the defending Stanley Cup champion Anaheim Ducks. If you weren't there, you probably could have been. The announced crowd of 17,610 was well below Joe Louis Arena's 20,066 capacity. Despite a great start to the season, the Wings continued to play before less-than-capacity crowds.

AULD LANG SYNE

OCTOBER-NOVEMBER: Robert Lang made it tough for the Wings to forget their old friend. He helped Chicago to a couple of come-from-behind victories over Detroit early in the season. The Wings started 0-3-1 against the Blackhawks, before winning two of the final three meetings.

START ME UP

OCTOBER-NOVEMBER: Henrik Zetterberg set a club record with at least a point in the first 17 games of the season. He beat the previous record of 14 set by Norm Ullman in 1960-61.

START ME UP II

OCTOBER-NOVEMBER: The Wings tied a club record by winning nine games in a row. Included in the run was the team's first ever three-game sweep in western Canada — 3-2 at Vancouver on Oct. 28, 2-1 at Edmonton on Oct. 30 and 4-1 at Calgary on Nov. 1.

START ME UP III

OCTOBER-NOVEMBER: A 3-2 loss to the Blackhawks on Nov. 11 ended the nine-game winning streak and snapped Chris Osgood's 20-game win streak without a regulation loss.

PROSPECT LOST

AMY LEANG

The Wings had hoped Igor Grigorenko would be a star for them. Instead, he came into training camp out of shape and never impressed. Grigorenko went back to Russia, where a player can make millions playing in the Russian Super League.

MORE THAN $1

OCT. 26: Kris Draper, acquired from Winnipeg for $1 in 1993, signed a three-year, $4.7-million extension. "It's not a secret how much I enjoy being part of the Red Wings and the organization," he said.

GOOD RIDDANCE

OCTOBER: Red Wings general manager Ken Holland made good on his promise to call up forward Igor Grigorenko before Nov. 1. Grigorenko, drafted 62nd overall in 2001, arrived out of shape and failed to impress during three weeks with the AHL's Grand Rapids Griffins, but Holland called him up anyway. Grigorenko had been considered one of the top prospects in hockey before an automobile accident cost him two years. Grigorenko returned to Russia a couple of days after his call-up, though. With Dallas Drake returning from an injury, the Wings preferred Matt Ellis' work ethic and Aaron Downey's toughness, so they demoted Grigorenko. Grigorenko, who stood to make more than $1 million by playing in the Russian Super League, decided to go home rather than take the demotion. By the end of the season, it was clear Grigorenko was no longer in the team's plans.

TWO IN FIVE

NOV. 24: Tomas Holmstrom and Pavel Datsyuk set a club record for fastest two goals before losing, 3-2, in a shoot-out to the Blue Jackets in Columbus. The Wings trailed, 2-0, in the second period when Holmstrom and Datsyuk scored five sec-

Both he and Kris Draper read political thrillers by Vince Flynn. There are card players like Andreas Lilja, Brett Lebda, Mikael Samuelsson and Dan Cleary, who play game after game of hearts.

MANDI WRIGHT

STARS ON ICE

The Wings had four All-Stars: Mike Babcock coached the Western Conference squad, which had Pavel Datsyuk, Henrik Zetterberg and Nicklas Lidstrom. Zetterberg did not play because of a bad back. Chris Osgood later was named an All-Star and started the game.

onds apart. That broke the record of seven seconds between goals, set twice, by Syd Howe and Larry Aurie against Toronto in 1936, and by Jeff Sharples and Brent Ashton against Winnipeg in 1987.

FIL'S FREEBIES

DECEMBER: Valtteri Filppula slipped a backhand penalty shot past Dan Ellis to give the Wings a 2-1 victory over the Predators in Nashville. It was the first penalty shot scored by a Wing in the regular season since Igor Larionov beat Sharks goaltender Arturs Irbe on Nov. 22, 1995. Larionov just happened to be in town on business and attended the game. Less than a week later, Filppula would net another goal on a penalty shot in a victory over the Florida Panthers at Joe Louis Arena. Filppula's goal came a few minutes after Pavel Datsyuk's penalty-shot attempt was denied by Tomas Vokoun. It was the first time in franchise history the Wings had two penalty shots in a game. Filppula became the first Wing since Steve Yzerman in 1992 to convert two penalty shots in a season.

KEEPING THE CAPTAIN

DEC. 26: Captain Nicklas Lidstrom agreed to a two-year, $15-million contract extension. "We knew Nick wasn't going to go anywhere," said coach Mike Babcock. "It's just how long does he want to play. ...

FRESH CHELI

AMY LEANG

On Jan. 8, Chris Chelios became the second-oldest player to appear in an NHL game "I always like it when fans yell at him that he should retire," Chris Osgood said. "It's giving him a compliment for being able to play for so long."

One day he's going to tell us he doesn't want to play. And we just hope it's not for a long, long time."

OH, WE'RE HALFWAY THERE

JAN. 3: The Wings' 30-8-3 start set an NHL record for best win total at the halfway point of an 82-game season. "Everyone in this locker room has one goal, and everyone knows what that is," Kris Draper said. "And you can't do that within the first 41 games."

OLDER THAN MOST

JAN. 8: Defenseman Chris Chelios became the oldest U.S.-born player and the second-oldest player overall in NHL history when he played in a 1-0 victory over the Avalanche. Chelios, who turned 46 on Jan. 25, passed Moe Roberts for second place at 45 years, 348 days. Chelios probably won't pass the oldest player, Wings Hall of Famer Gordie Howe, who retired for good at 52.

OZZIE NETS DEAL

JAN. 9: The Wings gave Chris Osgood, 19-2-1 with an NHL-leading 1.68 goals-against average at the time, a three-year contract extension worth about $1.5 million per season, nearly double the $800,000 he was making for the season.

STARRING WEEKEND

JAN. 26-27: Coach Mike Babcock, forward Pavel Datsyuk, defenseman Nicklas Lidstrom and goaltender Chris Osgood represented the Red Wings on the Western Conference team at the All-Star Game in Atlanta. Henrik Zetterberg was supposed to go, but he opted out to rest a sore back. Lidstrom was a minus-2 in the first period, and Osgood allowed five goals on 16 shots as the Eastern Conference beat the Western Conference, 8-7.

JAWBREAKER

FEB. 9: Dan Cleary, who already had matched his previous career highs of 20 goals and 20 assists set the previous season, suffered a broken jaw in the first period of a 3-2 loss in Toronto. Cleary missed 19 games — and lost 15 pounds while on a liquid diet. After months of negotiations, Cleary agreed to a five-year, $14-million contract. He was back to chewing normal foods and contributing on the ice before the start of the playoffs.

MANDI WRIGHT

WE CAN SEE CLEARY NOW

Dan Cleary, chatting with Darren McCarty, suffered a broken jaw Feb. 9. He returned in late March, but still couldn't feel his chin when he shaves. His jaw ached when he yawned, he couldn't eat a steak. But he was rewarded with a five-year extension worth $14 million.

WORST SLIDE SINCE '91

FEB. 7-17: The Wings lost six straight for the first time since losing seven in a row in January 1991. "When you've played as bad as we've played, it takes you awhile to crawl out of the mess you've made for yourself," Mike Babcock said. "We're all in this together. I think enough is enough."

CAPTAIN HURT IN COLORADO

FEB. 18: Ian Laperriere sent Wings captain Nicklas Lidstrom into the boards with a monstrous check six minutes into a game in Denver. Aaron Downey would pay Laperriere back, pounding him until he crouched down on the ice late in the first period. The Wings beat the Avs, 4-0, snapping their six-game losing streak. Lidstrom missed six games — the Wings were 2-3-1 without him — with a sprained medial collateral ligament.

FEBRUARY FLOP

In the middle of February, the Wings lost six straight and also lost Nicklas Lidstrom to a knee injury for three weeks. The Wings also struggled with injuries to Dominik Hasek, Brian Rafalski and Niklas Kronwall.

KIRTHMON F. DOZIER

AMY LEANG

AT THE HELM

During the '08 playoffs, the Wings' fourth line largely was anchored by Darren Helm, a 21-year-old rookie who entered the playoffs with seven NHL games. The Wings drafted Helm 132nd in 2005, again demonstrating a knack for finding late-round gems.

AMY LEANG

BANKING ON BRAD

The Wings decided Brad Stuart was the best, and cheapest, way to improve. He became a good partner for Niklas Kronwall who can hit and play with the puck.

ADDITION TO THE D

FEB. 26: The Red Wings bolstered an already-strong defensive corps by acquiring Brad Stuart from Los Angeles for a second-round pick in 2008 and a fourth-round pick in 2009. Stuart, known for his abrasive play, gave the Wings another big-hitting defenseman to go along with Niklas Kronwall. Stuart suffered a non-displaced broken finger in March, but was at full health for the playoffs.

AT THE HELM

MARCH 13: Darren Helm, who has drawn comparisons to Wings veteran Kris Draper, made his NHL debut against the Dallas Stars. Helm replaced Draper, who was out with a groin injury. "One day he's going to take my job," Draper said. "I'm just glad I signed that three-year deal. He's a great skater. Anytime you can skate, you give yourself an opportunity to play in this league." Helm, playing beyond his years, found regular ice time in the playoffs.

A NIGHT OF ACCOMPLISHMENT

MARCH 13: The Wings beat Dallas, 5-3, at Joe Louis Arena, clinching a playoff spot for the 17th consecutive season — the longest current streak in pro sports. The Wings also clinched the Central Division for the seventh consecutive season and reached 100 points for the eighth consecutive season, tying an NHL record set by the Montreal Canadiens (1974-75 to 1981-82).

50 AND BEST

MARCH 22: Wings coach Mike Babcock declared the current squad the best team he ever coached following a 4-1 victory over the Columbus Blue Jackets. The victory gave the Wings 50 wins for the third consecutive season, and Babcock became the first NHL coach to win at least 50 in the first three seasons with a team. "More depth, faster, harder, the will to win. Yeah, best team I ever coached," Babcock said.

MAC IS BACK

MARCH 28: Darren McCarty's successful comeback bid began with stints with the Flint Generals and Grand Rapids Griffins before he signed with the Wings. McCarty received a standing ovation as he played his first game as a Wing since May 3, 2004. McCarty opened the game on a line with former Grind Line mates Kris Draper and Kirk Maltby.

KIRTHMON F. DOZIER

MAC MAKES IT

Probably no athlete in Detroit sports history has publicly battled a series of demons as McCarty has. Alcohol. Marijuana. Gambling. Bankruptcy. Marital strife. But he still made a successful comeback to the Wings.

WINNING MULE

MARCH: Johan Franzen scored six game-winning goals in March, breaking the club record of five in a month shared by Gordie Howe (1952, 1956) and Henrik Zetterberg (2007). Franzen had 14 goals and four assists to earn the NHL's third star for the month. Franzen finished the season with career bests of 27 goals and 38 points.

A MR. HOCKEY AND A PREZ

APRIL 3: Michigan State junior forward Justin Abdelkader, who was the high school Mr. Hockey at Muskegon Mona Shores in 2004, made his NHL debut on the same night the Wings notched their record sixth Presidents' Trophy. The Blue Jackets took a 2-1 lead when a shot Abdelkader attempted to block got past him and Dominik Hasek. The Wings rallied to win, 3-2, and captain Nicklas Lidstrom handed Abdelkader the winning puck after the game.

PRESIDENT ZETTERBERG

JULIAN H. GONZALEZ

Several Wings mob Henrik Zetterberg after his game-winning goal with 12 seconds left April 3 captured the Presidents' Trophy for a record sixth time. No other club has won the trophy more than twice in the 22-year history of the award.

KOPECKY AND THE PREZ

APRIL 3: The Wings paid a price with their Presidents' Trophy. Tomas Kopecky, who missed the 2006-07 playoffs with a broken clavicle, suffered a torn medial collateral ligament and a sprained anterior cruciate ligament in the third period. Kopecky, leading Wings forwards with 111 hits at the time of his injury, underwent surgery in Birmingham, Ala., on April 22. He needs four to six months of rehab.

GOALIES SHARE >>

APRIL: Dominik Hasek and Chris Osgood won the Jennings Trophy, given to goalkeepers who play a minimum of 25 games for the team that allows the fewest goals. Osgood won the Jennings with Mike Vernon in 1995-96. Hasek had previously won the Jennings in 1993-94 and in 2000-01 with the Buffalo Sabres.

DATSYUK JOINS ELITE

APRIL: Pavel Datsyuk joined Gordie Howe and Steve Yzerman as the only players to lead the Wings in scoring for three consecutive seasons. Datsyuk scored 31 goals and led the team with 66 assists and 97 points in 82 games. Datsyuk led the Wings with 87 points in 2005-06 and 2006-07.

MANDI WRIGHT

THE SEASON
AROUND THE NHL

NEW SWEATERS, NO SWEAT   MADALYN RUGGIERO

New jerseys from Reebok weren't a hit early. The company made some adjustments after complaints about an inability to absorb sweat.

THE LEAGUE

BY GEORGE SIPPLE

Things to remember about the 2007-08 season:

500 CLUB

New Jersey's Martin Brodeur notched his 500th career win, joining Patrick Roy as the only NHL goaltenders to reach that plateau.

GM HULLY

Former Red Wing Brett Hull joined Les Jackson as co-general managers of the Stars on Nov. 11 after Doug Armstrong was fired, and led the Stars to the conference finals.

BIG 60

Alexander Ovechkin became the first player to score 60 goals since Pittsburgh's Mario Lemieux (69) and Jaromir Jagr (62) in 1995-96.

5 CLUB

Marian Gaborik of the Wild scored five goals in a 6-3 victory over the Rangers on Dec. 20. Sergei Fedorov, then with the Wings, had been the last player to score five goals in a game, on Dec. 26, 1996, against the Capitals.

JUST DUCKY

After leading the Anaheim Ducks to a Stanley Cup, Scott Niedermayer and Teemu Selanne took an extended vacation, then joined the team midway through the season. Some thought the Ducks were finding a creative way around the salary cap.

BLOODY MESS

Panthers forward Richard Zednik had an artery in his neck sliced by the skate of teammate Olli Jokinen in a game against the Sabres on Feb. 10. Zednik skated off the ice, but left a trail of blood.

GO OUTSIDE AND PLAY

The Sabres and Penguins played before an NHL-record crowd of 71,217 at Ralph Wilson Stadium on Jan. 1, 2008, in the league's second-ever regular-season game outdoors. The Penguins won, 2-1, in a shoot-out.

FINAL STANDINGS

WESTERN CONFERENCE

CENTRAL	GP	W	LOL	PTS	GF	GA	PP%	PK%	HOME	AWAY
1.Detroit	82	54	21 7	115	257	184	20.7	84.0	29-9-3	25-12-4
8.Nashville	82	41	32 9	91	230	229	14.8	85.4	23-14-4	18-18-5
Chicago	82	40	34 8	88	239	235	15.9	82.1	23-16-2	17-18-6
Columbus	82	34	36 12	80	193	218	14.9	83.3	20-14-7	14-22-5
St. Louis	82	33	36 13	79	205	237	14.1	84.4	20-15-6	13-21-7
NORTHWEST	GP	W	LOL	PTS	GF	GA	PP%	PK%	HOME	AWAY
3.Minnesota	82	44	28 10	98	223	218	18.9	85.2	25-11-5	19-17-5
6.Colorado	82	44	31 7	95	231	219	14.6	81.4	27-12-2	17-19-5
7.Calgary	82	42	30 10	94	229	227	16.8	81.4	21-11-9	21-19-1
Edmonton	82	41	35 6	88	235	251	16.6	84.7	23-17-1	18-18-5
Vancouver	82	39	33 10	88	213	215	17.1	82.6	21-15-5	18-18-5
PACIFIC	GP	W	LOL	PTS	GF	GA	PP%	PK%	HOME	AWAY
2.San Jose	82	49	23 10	108	222	193	18.8	85.8	22-13-6	27-10-4
4.Anaheim	82	47	27 8	102	205	191	16.6	83.1	28-9-4	19-18-4
5.Dallas	82	45	30 7	97	242	207	18.1	85.5	23-16-2	22-14-5
Phoenix	82	38	37 7	83	214	231	18.6	80.7	17-20-4	21-17-3
Los Angeles	82	32	43 7	71	231	266	17.5	78.1	17-21-3	15-22-4

EASTERN CONFERENCE

ATLANTIC	GP	W	LOL	PTS	GF	GA	PP%	PK%	HOME	AWAY
2.Pittsburgh	82	47	27 8	102	247	216	20.4	81.0	26-10-5	21-17-3
4.New Jersey	82	46	29 7	99	206	197	15.6	82.8	25-14-2	21-15-5
5.NY Rangers	82	42	27 13	97	213	199	16.5	84.5	25-13-3	17-14-10
6.Philadelphia	82	42	29 11	95	248	233	21.8	83.2	21-14-6	21-15-5
NY Islanders	82	35	38 9	79	194	243	14.5	81.9	18-18-5	17-20-4
NORTHEAST	GP	W	LOL	PTS	GF	GA	PP%	PK%	HOME	AWAY
1.Montreal	82	47	25 10	104	262	222	24.2	82.5	22-13-6	25-12-4
7.Ottawa	82	43	31 8	94	261	247	18.3	81.1	22-15-4	21-16-4
8.Boston	82	41	29 12	94	212	222	17.6	78.6	21-16-4	20-13-8
Buffalo	82	39	31 12	90	255	242	18.0	83.2	20-15-6	19-16-6
Toronto	82	36	35 11	83	231	260	17.8	78.0	18-17-6	18-18-5
SOUTHEAST	GP	W	LOL	PTS	GF	GA	PP%	PK%	HOME	AWAY
3.Washington	82	43	31 8	94	242	231	19.0	80.5	23-15-3	20-16-5
Carolina	82	43	33 6	92	252	249	18.8	78.8	24-13-4	19-20-2
Florida	82	38	35 9	85	216	226	19.2	82.4	18-15-8	20-20-1
Atlanta	82	34	40 8	76	216	272	16.5	78.8	19-19-3	15-21-5
Tampa Bay	82	31	42 9	71	223	267	19.3	81.9	20-18-3	11-24-6

SCORING

NAME	G	A	PTS	+/-	PIM
A. Ovechkin, WAS	65	47	112	28	40
Evgeni Malkin, PIT	47	59	106	16	78
Jarome Iginla, CGY	50	48	98	27	83
Pavel Datsyuk, DET	**31**	**66**	**97**	**41**	**20**
Joe Thornton, SJ	29	67	96	18	59
H. Zetterberg, DET	**43**	**49**	**92**	**30**	**34**
V. Lecavalier, TB	40	52	92	-17	89
Jason Spezza, OTT	34	58	92	26	66
D. Alfredsson, OTT	40	49	89	15	34
Ilya Kovalchuk, ATL	52	35	87	-12	52

GOALTENDING

NAME	GP	W	LOTL	GAA	SV%	SO
Chris Osgood, DET	**43**	**27**	**9**	**4 2.09**	**.914**	**4**
J. Giguere, ANH	58	35	17	6 2.12	.922	4
Evgeni Nabokov, SJ	77	46	21	8 2.14	.910	6
Dominik Hasek, DET	**41**	**27**	**10**	**3 2.14**	**.902**	**5**
Martin Brodeur, NJ	77	44	27	6 2.17	.920	4
Henrik Lundqvist, NYR	72	37	24	10 2.23	.912	10
Pascal Leclaire, CLS	54	24	17	6 2.25	.919	9
Niklas Backstrom, MIN	58	33	13	8 2.31	.920	4
Marty Turco, DAL	62	32	21	6 2.32	.909	3
C. Huet, MON/WAS	52	32	14	6 2.32	.920	4

TEAM SCORING

Ottawa 3.15
Montreal 3.13
Detroit 3.07
Buffalo 3.06
Carolina 3.05

TEAM GOALS AGAINST

Detroit 2.18
Anaheim 2.24
San Jose 2.28
NY Rangers . 2.32
New Jersey . 2.35

THE SCENE

AMY LEANG

FAMILY TRIP

Red Wings forward Pavel Datsyuk signs Ian Springfield's poster outside the team hotel in Pittsburgh. Ian, 11, is wearing his No. 13 jersey - Datsyuk's jersey. When the Wings clinched their berth in the Stanley Cup finals, Ian's father, Scott, booked a hotel in Pittsburgh. He pulled Ian and sister Emma, 9, out of school. The family was making hockey memories in honor of his late wife and mother Kim, who played hockey for women's recreation leagues in Mt. Clemens and Troy.

AMY LEANG

BARING IT ALL

Pumped-up face painters ruled at Joe Louis Arena. The Doran brothers of Allen Park represented with their own individual red and white designs, which were topped off by chest paintings, courtesy of their aunt. David Doran, 21, right, had the Stanley Cup painted on his chest with an optimistic "2008." Daniel, 19, had the cup with "2002"; Dylan, 15, had the cup with "1998," and Derek, 13, had the cup with "1997." "We get pretty pumped," said David Doran, a senior at Northland Baptist College in Wisconsin.

JULIAN H. GONZALEZ

BETTER THAN PITT

Chris Osgood wasn't just good on the ice. He had numerous fans off it. Actress and Michigan native Kristen Bell ("Veronica Mars") said she once had a crush on the Wings goalie. "Brad Pitt be damned, he had nothing on Osgood's rookie skill and sad eyes," she told NHL.com.

AMY LEANG

HOCKEYTOWN A HIT AGAIN

Red Wings fans cheer as Tomas Holmstrom knocks a Pittsburgh player into the boards during Game 2 of the finals. In 2006-07, the Wings' TV ratings were down, and had been for years. Ticket sales were decreasing. Empty seats were everywhere. But in 2008, ticket sales and TV ratings went up, and, for the first time in years, Wings chatter on the radio isn't an invitation to turn the dial. It also helped that ticket prices fell between 18% and 36%.

THE BIG MAN AT THE JOE

Zamboni driver (and octopus twirler) Al Sobotka sends a cephalopod soaring at the Joe. At one point, the NHL announced that it would fine anyone $10,000 if they twirled an octopus over their head. The reason: "Matter flies off the octopus and gets on the ice when (someone) does it."

DIANE WEISS

CHAPTER THREE

THE TEAM

The Wings are a model of United Nations integration. Their success is a result of on-ice dominance and off-ice chemistry. In a room stocked with stars from around the world, success is bred because egos are pushed aside for the common good. Dominik Hasek didn't play after being pulled in Game 4 of Round 1, but rather than sulk about losing his status as a starter, he rooted for Chris Osgood.

The camaraderie shines through on the road and at home.

"We're team-oriented quite a bit," Osgood said. "There are a lot of different personalities and a lot of different nationalities, and on some teams you see the Swedes only hang out with each other, or the Russians, but we all stick together as one. It's unseen from the outside, but we all get along, and that's something that's important for when we go on the ice."

JULIAN H. GONZALEZ

TOUGH CHIN
It's not easy to tell whether Mike Babcock is being funny, sarcastic or cocky. He isn't above making mistakes or admitting to them.

JULIAN H. GONZALEZ

HOCKEYTOWN HERO
MIKE BABCOCK, COACH

Mr. Anonymous

WINGS' OLD-SCHOOL COACH REMAINS UNDER THE RADAR

BY MITCH ALBOM

He has come a long way in 20 years, when he was skating for a British hockey team while teaching at a local college.

"Did you ever come to class with a black eye?" I asked Mike Babcock.

"Probably," he said.

You can't get much more anonymous than the Whitley Warriors, near Newcastle upon Tyne, where Babcock, between classes, played in "a barn that sat 5,000 people" and had a mesh screen instead of glass, so the puck bounced off it.

But fast-forward two decades, to Babcock's current existence. He lives in plain sight — on a suburban street in Northville, his house looking like the others to the left and right. He picks up his kids at school and might drive them to soccer or ballet. He goes to their games, eats around town.

Mike Babcock lives his life in Michigan pretty much like everyone else, which is to be expected if you are everyone else — but not when you are coach of the Red Wings.

22 FOREVER HOCKEYTOWN
THE TEAM

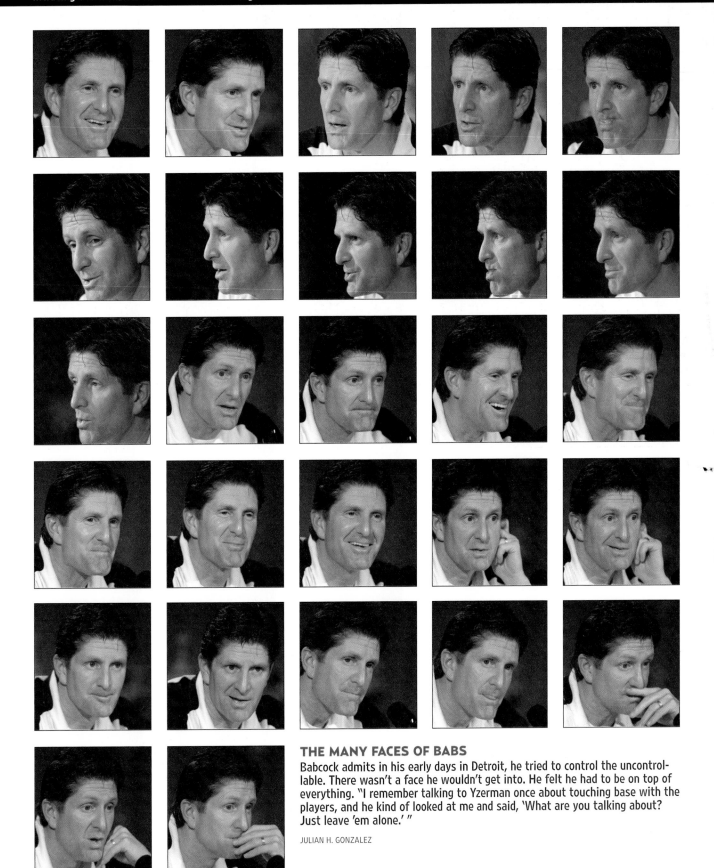

THE MANY FACES OF BABS
Babcock admits in his early days in Detroit, he tried to control the uncontrollable. There wasn't a face he wouldn't get into. He felt he had to be on top of everything. "I remember talking to Yzerman once about touching base with the players, and he kind of looked at me and said, 'What are you talking about? Just leave 'em alone.' "

JULIAN H. GONZALEZ

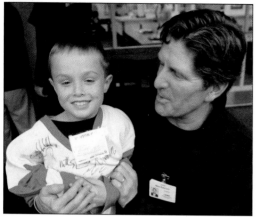

CHARITABLE COACH
Mike Babcock, who donates two tickets to each game to a child battling cancer, spent some time at Children's Hospital of Michigan. "I have kids here all the time," Babcock said. "You need to be reminded how lucky you are. I have three healthy children and am thankful every day that that's the case."

Where is the fuss? Coach of the Wings? Isn't that a superstar position? It was for Scotty Bowman, who won fewer games in his first three seasons in Detroit than Babcock has.

Answer this: What do you know about Mike Babcock?

Detroit fans know Tigers manager Jim Leyland's smoking habits and Lions coach Rod Marinelli's odd speech pattern. Babcock, 45, has been in Detroit as long as both of them, yet he remains under the radar.

In his first season, Babcock's Wings lost in the first round. Last season, they lost in the conference finals.

When it comes to hockey, fans like June parades, not May backslaps.

Babcock has seen June before. His first season as a coach in the NHL, 2002-03, he reached Game 7 of the Stanley Cup finals. His Ducks lost that night, 3-0, at New Jersey.

"When you think you're gonna lift that Cup and taste it ... and you don't get to touch it, you don't get to get near it, you just get to look at it."

Now, he gets to hold the Cup instead of watching someone else do it, and the relative anonymity he has lived under in Detroit has been shattered.

Now, there will be a rush of interest in the man who finally did what they have all been waiting for since Bowman — the man who only six years ago wasn't even coaching in this league and who only 20 years ago was smashing Brits into the boards on weekends and teaching during the week.

TOUGH GUY
Kirk Maltby, to the Associated Press about how Babcock changed the Wings: "I don't want to say there was a lot of yelling, but our practices were a lot more intense and he was much more vocal. I don't think he's changed. He's still very much about preparation and his system."

AMY LEANG

POINTING THEM IN THE RIGHT DIRECTION
Babcock has preached driving to the net to score, digging in the corners for pucks and punishing players in open ice. He changed the Wings' style of play, and it paid off, maximizing the talent on the roster and creating roles for other players.

THE BABCOCK FILE

THE BIO
AGE: 45
FROM: Saskatoon, Saskatchewan

THE HISTORY
Won 231 regular-season games — and two Presidents' Trophies (both with Wings) — in five seasons as NHL coach.

THE STATS

2002-03
MIGHTY DUCKS

40-27-9-6

STANDINGS: 95 points, second in Pacific Division.
PLAYOFFS: Lost to Devils in Stanley Cup finals.

2003-04
MIGHTY DUCKS

29-35-10-8

STANDINGS: 76 points, fourth in Pacific Division.
PLAYOFFS: None.

2005-06
RED WINGS

58-16-8

STANDINGS: 124 points, first in NHL.
PLAYOFFS: Lost to Oilers in first round.

2006-07
RED WINGS

50-19-13

STANDINGS: 113 points, tied for first in NHL.
PLAYOFFS: Lost to Ducks in Western finals.

2007-08
RED WINGS

54-21-7

STANDINGS: 115 points, first in NHL.
PLAYOFFS: Won Stanley Cup.

HOCKEYTOWN HERO
HENRIK ZETTERBERG, LEFT WING

Next superstar

MEET THE NEW KING OF HOCKEY IN Z-TROIT

BY MITCH ALBOM

The first time Henrik Zetterberg set foot in Joe Louis Arena, the Red Wings were in the playoffs against Colorado. He was a new draftee; he wore a suit, and he felt like an idiot.

"Who wears a suit at a hockey game?" he recalls thinking.

Afterward, he and Niklas Kronwall, another Detroit pick, were ushered into the locker room to meet the team. They felt awkward, like forced guests at someone else's party. Luckily, the game had been won, and the players were friendly.

So he and Kronwall came back the next game. This time, Detroit lost. And the locker room "was like a funeral; even guys' families were upset."

Zetterberg got a taste of what the playoffs are about — how you put your heart on the line every night. In the 2007-08 season, he got the ultimate firsthand exposure in the Stanley Cup finals. Like Pittsburgh's Sidney Crosby, it was his first time.

Crosby might be "the new face of the NHL," but Zetterberg could be.

This is a kid who is rock-star good-looking, has a high-profile girlfriend, mad skills, a humble demeanor and a knack for finding the puck as if he and it were separated at birth. His numbers are at superstar levels. He makes everyone around him better. He's fast, dynamic, tough on defense and has an almost cosmic connection with linemate Pavel Datsyuk.

JULIAN H. GONZALEZ

A GOOD LOOK
The Wings drafted Zetterberg in the seventh round in 1999. They had no idea he would make it to the NHL. They also had no way to gauge his will. "That's where he's like Stevie (Yzerman)," GM Ken Holland said. "It's the will. Few people have it."

Zetterberg, 27, is no stranger to media, interviews or outside curiosity. In his native Sweden, Zetterberg and his girlfriend of two years, Emma Andersson — a Swedish model and TV celebrity — are photographed constantly. Dinners are regularly interrupted, and stories get written.

When they return to America, they revel in the relative anonymity. "We like being normal people," he says.

Zetterberg never dreamed of fame in the NHL.

Z-TROIT

No player in Hockeytown epitomizes Detroit more than the scrawny, seventh-round pick from Sweden. "You have to win to become a star," he said during the season, "and I haven't won yet." Until now.

JULIAN H. GONZALEZ

THE ZETTERBERG FILE

THE BIO

AGE: 27

FROM: Njurunda, Sweden

HT/WT: 5-11, 195

EXP.: Fifth season

DRAFTED: By Red Wings, 1999, Round 7, No. 210 overall

2008 SALARY: $2.7 million.

THE STATS

GAMES ... 75		PIM 34
GOALS ... 43		PP PTS .. 36
ASSISTS .. 49		SH PTS 1
POINTS ... 92		SHOTS .. 358
+/- 30		SHOT% .. 12.0

THE ROLE

Zetterberg is easily one of the best two-way forwards and a constant scoring threat with his excellent speed, agility and stickhandling abilities. He is equally adept as a passer and considered a special talent with the ability to make teammates better.

THE HISTORY

■ Led rookies in goals (22) and points (44) in 2002-03, finishing second in voting to Blues defenseman Barret Jackman for the Calder Trophy, given to the NHL's rookie of the year.
■ Led Sweden to the gold medal in the 2006 Winter Olympics.

DID YOU KNOW?

Played soccer growing up, but only in the summer when it was too warm to play hockey. What he misses most about Sweden: Sibylla, a chain of hot dog/hamburger stands.

QUOTABLE

"As long as Detroit is willing, I'll sign (with them) for the rest of my career."

ZETTERBERG, on his future with the Wings.

NOT A REACH

JULIAN H. GONZALEZ

Despite his 5-foot-11, 195-pound frame, Zetterberg is a relentless, defensive-minded point machine, plays with the sort of grit perfectly suited to Detroit's blue-collar ethos and has forced himself into the MVP conversation. He was also a candidate, along with Pavel Datsyuk, for the Selke Trophy.

Now, team officials are banking on it. Whenever you talk marketing, they gush about Zetterberg. And they wonder why he isn't already a household heartthrob.

Part of that is because he joined the Wings (2002-03 season) when you had to get in line to be a Hall of Famer.

Yet for a guy who knows how to be cautious in an interview, Zetterberg can be surprisingly candid.

When asked how he thought he would feel if he won the Stanley Cup this year, he avoided the standard "dream come true" stuff and instead evoked a previous feeling of ennui.

"When we won the Olympics" — in 2006, playing for Sweden — "the feeling was kind of like, 'Is this it?' That game was so mentally tough, that when it was over, you won, and then it was like" — he exhales — "you were so empty. You were empty. You were happy, but at the same time, I thought it would be more.

"On the other hand, when I first got here we had that great team, and we lost in the first round. The next year we lost in the second round. That feeling you have after the last game of the year when you're not on the winning side, it's like, 'My God.' It's so mentally tough.

"So I don't know what the feeling would be like to win a Cup. But I know I don't want to have the feeling you have when you lose. It's the worst."

Nothing cliché about that, is there?

Zetterberg has blossomed with every passing year.

The team loves him. Management loves him. Fans love him. It seems a cinch that he will one day take over as captain when Nicklas Lidstrom retires.

Zetterberg might not want to be the face of the NHL, but he might not have a choice.

JULIAN H. GONZALEZ

BALANCING ACT

Pavel Datsyuk has shown for years how incredibly talented he is with the puck. He finished the 2007-08 season with 97 points. But 2007-08 also was the first season his defensive prowess matched his offensive skill. Datsyuk led the NHL with a plus-41, one better than teammate Nicklas Lidstrom.

HOCKEYTOWN HERO
PAVEL DATSYUK, CENTER

Master P

RED WINGS' TOP SCORER IS PART POET, PART PUGILIST

BY HELENE ST. JAMES

MANDI WRIGHT

When Pavel Datsyuk learned in 2002 what it felt like to win the Stanley Cup, he compared the emotion to seeing a beautiful sunrise.

Then, Datsyuk was 23 and an NHL rookie, albeit a clearly talented one, so much so even the notoriously picky Brett Hull adored playing with him.

In 2008, Datsyuk was an alpha forward and a key reason the Red Wings won another Cup.

Datsyuk has shown for years how incredibly talented he is on offense. He finished the 2007-08 season with 97 points. But 2008 was the first season his defensive prowess matched his offensive skill. Datsyuk led the NHL with a plus-41, one better than teammate Nicklas Lidstrom. For the first time, Datsyuk was a regular penalty killer.

He blossomed, in general manager Ken Holland's words, into "a superstar." Datsyuk wasn't just a fun player or creator. He was one of the world's best.

Datsyuk jumped up his physical game, too.

When 6-foot-4, 224-pound Penguins forward Ryan Malone went after Datsyuk's linemate, Henrik Zetterberg, giving him an extra push after a whistle in Game 2 of the Cup finals, Datsyuk got in Malone's face and exchanged shoves. At the tail end of the game, it was Datsyuk who threw a couple of rights after Penguins forward Gary Roberts went after him.

"It's a part of the game," Datsyuk said. "I have lots of text messages from Russian fans who watch."

MORE WORK
Pavel Datsyuk has developed into a penalty killer. "He's gotten more responsibility," Nicklas Lidstrom said. "He's out there killing penalties, where he wasn't before. That makes him think a lot more about his defensive play. You have to be in the right spot. You can't cheat or cut corners."

THE DATSYUK FILE

THE BIO

AGE: 29
FROM: Yekaterinburg, Russia
HT/WT: 5-11, 194
EXP.: Sixth season
DRAFTED: By Red Wings, 1998, Round 6, No. 171 overall
2008 SALARY: $6.7 million
NICKNAMES: Pavs, Dats and Moves

THE STATS

GAMES	82	PIM	20
GOALS	31	PP PTS	40
ASSISTS	66	SH PTS	1
POINTS	97	SHOTS	264
+/-	41	SHOT %	11.7

THE ROLE

Datsyuk's blend of speed, skill and grit makes him a valuable NHL commodity and a franchise cornerstone. He not only finished in the top five in assists and points but is widely considered one of the league's top defensive forwards. His 144 takeaways were more than 50 clear of his closest competitor. The combination of Datsyuk and Henrik Zetterberg gives the Wings one of the league's most potent scoring tandems.

THE HISTORY

■ Wasn't chosen in the 1996 or 1997 NHL drafts.
■ Seven-year contract ($46.9 million) he signed in 2007 was the longest extension in club history.

THE HONORS

Won Lady Byng Trophy in 2006 and 2007. The award is presented to the player who displays the best sportsmanship and gentlemanly conduct combined with on-ice performance. Also a Lady Byng finalist in 2008. Was a finalist for the 2008 Selke Trophy, given each year to the best defensive forward.

QUOTABLE

"I'm a big star now."

PAVEL DATSYUK, after learning he'd been selected to start for the Western Conference All-Star team in 2007-08.

STAR PRAISE
Said Dallas goaltender Marty Turco of Datsyuk: "The hands, the feet, the moves ... they're magical. I played at the University of Michigan, so I know that sports are like a religion in Detroit, and I don't think those Detroit fans have seen magic like that since, well, uh ..." Barry Sanders, maybe? "Perfect," said Turco.

JULIAN H. GONZALEZ

STEPHEN MCGEE

DATS IS GOOD

Pavel Datsyuk loves golf. But he doesn't like speaking too much. Even though he has played for the Wings since 2001-02, Datsyuk isn't totally comfortable giving interviews in English. Datsyuk doesn't say much, but nobody cares. He is too good. Speaking is optional.

Datsyuk was making a joke about his punching tendencies coinciding with the rise of Russian boxers.

Little tidbits like that are why the Wings speak so highly about how Datsyuk is in the locker room, where he is considered one of the funniest guys on the team.

"Pavel is hilarious," defenseman Niklas Kronwall said. "When his English gets even better, I think people around the league will find out, too. His sense of humor is really great, sometimes very, very dry."

Datsyuk's English remains heavily accented seven years after he left his native Russia. He hails from Yekaterinburg, a big industrial city in central Russia most famous as the site where, in 1918, Tsar Nicholas II and his wife and children were executed by the Bolsheviks. Ninety years later, the city counts Datsyuk as a notable citizen, one whose fame has reached new heights this season.

His defense grew so dominant, he was, together with Zetterberg, a finalist for the Selke Trophy as the NHL's best defensive forward.

MANDI WRIGHT

D-ATSYUK

Datsyuk always faces the opponent's top line when at home, and he draws the opponent's top defensemen on the road. He said his defense has improved "because, every year, I have more experience, and I like taking puck from other player." Teammate Niklas Kronwall suggested Datsyuk's emergence as a top two-way player tied into being named an alternate captain in 2007-08.

H O C K E Y T O W N   H E R O
CHRIS OSGOOD, GOALTENDER

Wizard of Oz

OZZIE RETURNS TO WINGS AND BECOMES BETTER THAN EVER

BY MICHAEL ROSENBERG

C hris Osgood had just broken Terry Sawchuk's club record for postseason wins, and he was the one who brought it up in the postgame news conference. It's possible nobody else in the room would have asked.

Osgood wasn't the story in the 4-1 win over the Dallas Stars that sent the Red Wings back to the Stanley Cup finals. When the Wings win, he never is.

Give the man his due. But first, let's give him his stage.

"That was one of my goals, among others," Osgood said of the record. "It was a special night for me. But we got our team back to the Stanley Cup finals. That's most important."

Osgood became a viable candidate for the Conn Smythe Trophy as playoffs MVP for the Cup champions, but some people think any goalie can compete for the Cup behind the talented Wings. History has shown otherwise.

HE WINS
Osgood has never claimed to be the reason the Wings won. He just wants to be part of the victories. Some people seem to think any goalie can compete for the Cup behind the talented Wings, and history has shown that isn't true. Ask Curtis Joseph. Ask Manny Legace.

JULIAN H. GONZALEZ

THE OSGOOD FILE

THE BIO

AGE: 35

FROM: Peace River, Alberta

HT/WT: 5-10, 178

EXP: 15th season

DRAFTED: By Red Wings, 1991, Round 3, No. 54 overall

2008 SALARY: $800,000

THE STATS

GAMES	43	OTL	4
WINS	27	GAA	2.09
LOSSES	9	SV%	.914

THE ROLE

After sharing the spotlight with other goalies during two stints in Detroit, Osgood emerged as the No. 1 goalie in the first round of the '08 playoffs when Dominik Hasek struggled. Returned to the All-Star Game after a 10-year hiatus when coach Mike Babcock named him the starter.

THE HISTORY

- Three-time Stanley Cup winner with Wings.
- Starting skating at age 4.

THE AWARDS

Shared Jennings Trophy (lowest regular-season GAA) twice ('96 with Mike Vernon, '08 with Hasek).

QUOTABLE

"I've never been a guy that needs 40 shots to feel good. I think I can play well in any situation, whether it's 15 shots or 30 shots or whatever."

OSGOOD, on how he fits into the Wings' puck-possession style of play.

SMILE AND SAVE

Chris Osgood, with Wings food server Leslie Winfield-Baker and Kris Draper, cannot help that he looks, at 35, like he's still in high school. His cherubic features have always shaded him more Ricky Schroder than Gump Worsley.

KIMBERLY P. MITCHELL

COMEBACK

When the Wings told Osgood they didn't want him in Detroit anymore, he refused to accept a departure. He kept a home here and viewed his time in New York and St. Louis as an exile. Eventually, Detroit brought him back.

AMY LEANG

MANDI WRIGHT

FAMILY MAN

Osgood lives in Plymouth, a family town, in a family house on a family street with his family; wife Jenna and daughters Mackenzie and Sydney. His backyard contains a hockey oval that is frozen in the winter.

Ask Curtis Joseph. He couldn't handle the pressure. Joseph came to Detroit to be the hero, but he wasn't prepared for days it didn't happen.

Ask Manny Legace. He became an All-Star with St. Louis, but he couldn't carry the Wings in the playoffs.

After Legace struggled in the 2005-06 postseason, the Wings announced they didn't know who their goalie would be the next season.

"There has always been this perception that we won because of our skill and lost because of our goaltending," general manager Ken Holland said.

One reason Wings fans don't appreciate their goalies more is the team's puck-possession style. It doesn't give goalies many chances to be a hero.

Some goalies say it's easier to concentrate when they face a lot of shots, but Osgood said, "I've never been a guy that needs 40 shots to feel good."

Osgood probably lost his chance at being a true Detroit icon June 3, 1998. That was when he gave up a goal on a 90-foot shot to Dallas' Jamie Langenbrunner in overtime of Game 5 of the Western finals.

But what about what happened next? If ever there was a time to choke, that was it. Osgood had given up one of the most embarrassing goals in team history, a year after another Wings goalie, Mike Vernon, had won the Conn Smythe.

Yet Osgood pitched a shutout in Game 6 to clinch a trip to the finals, where he started all four games in a sweep of the Capitals in the Cup finals.

Said teammate Kris Draper: "I've never seen him as focused and determined. Everyone who knows him is happy for him."

HOCKEYTOWN HERO
NICKLAS LIDSTROM, DEFENSEMAN

'C' of change

LIDSTROM BECOMES FIRST EURO CAPTAIN TO WIN CUP

BY HELENE ST. JAMES

Steve Yzerman always was sure of one thing when the Red Wings faced a challenge: Nicklas Lidstrom would provide nothing but excellence.

When they were teammates, Yzerman relied on Lidstrom to anchor the defense, make big plays and contain opposing forwards. Those attributes, along with an unflappable demeanor, made Lidstrom a natural to succeed Yzerman as captain two years ago and become the first European born-and-bred player to captain his team to the Stanley Cup.

Lidstrom, from Sweden, just finished playing in his fifth Stanley Cup finals. The last time he was in the finals, in 2002, he became the first European to win the Conn Smythe Trophy as playoffs MVP.

Those who have known him longest — Yzerman, general manager Ken Holland and ex-coach Scotty Bowman — see Lidstrom as having all the qualities that make a great leader.

"I think he's unflappable," Holland said. "I don't think there's anything that's going to rattle him. He's easygoing and on a real even keel, and then you add in 15 or 16 years of experience; you're even more unflappable because of the experiences you've been through."

Bowman, a team consultant since retiring from coaching in 2002, has seen subtle changes in Lidstrom since he went from being an alternate to captain.

"He's more assertive now," Bowman said. "He knows his place as a leader."

JULIAN H. GONZALEZ

UNFLAPPABLE
Selected by Detroit 53rd overall in the 1989 NHL entry draft, Lidstrom had 49 assists in 80 games of the 1991-92 season, setting a club record by a rookie defenseman.

While he was captain, Yzerman often asked Lidstrom if a second opinion was needed.

"He was somebody I always relied on," Yzerman said. "I knew I could always go to him and run something by him, because I had great respect for his opinion and his insight."

Lidstrom serves a similar role now for Mike Babcock.

"He's won three Cups. He's won Olympics and world championships," said the coach. "I still think it's a little bit different this time, having this opportunity when you're the captain, and no European player has ever been able to do it."

Lidstrom is a candidate again to win the Norris Trophy as the NHL's top defenseman; if so, it would be his sixth in seven years. But long before he was recognized nationally, he was appreciated locally by his former captain.

"He had an immediate impact as a rookie, right from game one, and really since 1997, he's been the most dominant defenseman in the league," Yzerman said.

THE LIDSTROM FILE

THE BIO

AGE: 38.

FROM: Vasteras, Sweden

HT/WT: 6-1, 193

EXP: 16th season

DRAFTED: By Red Wings, 1989, Round 3, No. 53 overall

2008 SALARY: $7.6 million

STATS

GAMES	76	PIM	40
GOALS	10	PP PTS	34
ASSISTS	60	SH PTS	1
POINTS	70	SHOTS	188
+/-	40	SHOT%	.053

THE ROLE

Lidstrom's value to the team is almost immeasurable. He's arguably the best defenseman in the NHL and a leader by example who always seems to make the right play at the right time.

THE HISTORY

■ Known for his durability, consistently ranks amongst the top in the NHL in ice time.

■ In Sweden, he is known by his nickname "Lidas" (pronounced 'LEE-duss").

THE AWARDS

Fourth player to win Norris Trophy as NHL's top defenseman at least five times, and the first European to win it. First European to win the Conn Smythe Trophy (2001-02) as MVP of the Stanley Cup playoffs.

DID YOU KNOW?

Played soccer as a kid.

QUOTABLE

"I think he's unflappable. I don't think there's anything that's going to rattle him."

KEN HOLLAND,
Wings general manager, on Lidstrom's presence as captain.

SWEDISH HOSPITALITY   JULIAN H. GONZALEZ

Lidstrom and his wife, Annika, have four sons, ranging from 14 to 5. In 2006, at their Northville home, Lidstrom turned the backyard tennis court into a hockey rink.

CALM, COOL, COLLECTED

"I'm not going to try to be Steve Yzerman," Lidstrom said when he took over as Wings captain. "I've got to be myself. I'm not going to try to change. What I'm probably going to do is try to be more vocal in the room. But it's not like we have a young team -- we have a lot of veterans, so I don't think it's going to fall on one guy's shoulders to lead the whole team."

MANDI WRIGHT

SNAPSHOT

JULIAN H. GONZALEZ

Colorado forward Joe Sakic on Lidstrom: "He's one of those guys that probably drives everybody nuts because you can't beat him. It's more frustrating playing against a guy like Nicklas, who's in such good position you can't beat him, than if somebody tries to take a run at you. At least then you have a chance that maybe he misses you and you've got a shot on goal."

TROPHY CASE

Nicklas Lidstrom, posing with the 2008 Presidents' trophy for the best record in the league, is "so smart, he never gets hit, never hits, but is always in position and always ready to play," ex-Wing Paul Coffey said.

JULIAN H. GONZALEZ

AGED TO PERFECTION

Chelios: "Thank God I still have Dominik (Hasek) and Nick (Lidstrom). And guys like (Kris) Draper and (Kirk) Maltby, sometimes I feel like they're my age, they've been around so long. If it hadn't been for a few guys here like that, I think I would have moved on. That's what happened in Chicago. They went with a youth movement, and I felt really uncomfortable."

AMY LEANG

HOCKEYTOWN HERO
CHRIS CHELIOS, DEFENSEMAN

Aged to perfection

46-YEAR-OLD DEFENSEMAN KEEPS GOING AND GOING

BY MITCH ALBOM

The year he was born, Johnny Carson started on "The Tonight Show," John Glenn orbited the Earth in a spacecraft, and the U.S. discovered Soviet missile bases in Cuba.

Chris Chelios still is skating.

The year he started grade school, Dr. Christiaan Barnard performed the first heart transplant and actor Dustin Hoffman said, "Mrs. Robinson, you're trying to seduce me."

Chris Chelios still is skating.

He remembers fiddling with rabbit ears on a black-and-white TV. He remembers beers they served in his father's bar — like Schlitz and Hamm's — that are now hard to find.

He remembers 1969, when his father packed up the family in a Cadillac, drove to San Francisco and hopped on a boat that took 21 days to reach Australia. Chelios threw footballs with soldiers on leave from Vietnam.

Vietnam? Australia? Twenty-one days on a boat?

JULIAN H. GONZALEZ

CHELI CHAT
Chelios, right, talking to Valtteri Filppula, is the oldest U.S.-born player and second-oldest player in NHL history, trailing Gordie Howe, who retired at 52.

STEPHEN MCGEE

BIKING BODY

Chelios: "You have to prove yourself every day. If you have a bad week, they're going to say something about your age. ... Music is a pretty good indication of your age. The kids on the team never heard of any of my songs."

Chris Chelios still is skating.

"It is weird," said the 46-year-old Red Wings defenseman, the oldest player in the NHL.

"You can feel a little out of it sometimes. Because they're so young, it's hard to have conversations with a lot of guys on the team. I've started to develop better relations with the alumni."

Or maybe the alumni's parents. Chris Chelios is twice as old as some teammates. He is a year older than his coach!

Yet there he is, skating in these playoffs.

My guess is Valtteri Filppula has never owned the flare-bottom pants Chelios wore as a teenager, never had the mullet haircut he sported as a young player, never heard the disco music that played in the rinks where a young Chelios skated.

Chelios admits that when Steve Yzerman and Brendan Shanahan left after the 2006-07 season, "I lost a lot of my conversation.

"Thank God I still have Dominik (Hasek) and Nick (Lidstrom). And guys like (Kris) Draper and (Kirk) Maltby.

"If it hadn't been for a few guys here like that, I think I would have moved on."

He plays against guys only a few years older than his first-born son, who is 18.

During the season, Wings general manager Ken Holland told the media he wanted Chelios back for another year. When Chelios heard that, he says he felt good. Maybe even a bit younger.

He is a physical miracle and an encyclopedia of references most Wings have never heard of, from Alcatraz to ZZ Top.

CHIPPY CHELI

Chelios remains a solid penalty killer and aggravates like few others. As then-Sharks coach Ron Wilson said in 2007, when you go into the corner with Chelios, he's going to punch you in the head.

JULIAN H. GONZALEZ

THE CHELIOS FILE

THE BIO
AGE: 46
FROM: Chicago
HT/WT: 6-0, 191
EXPERIENCE: 23rd season
DRAFTED: By Montreal, 1981, Round 2, No. 40 overall
2008 SALARY: $850,000

STATS

GAMES ...	69
GOALS	3
ASSISTS ...	9
POINTS ...	12
+/-	11
PIM	36
PP PTS	0
SH PTS	0
SHOTS ...	60
SHOT% ...	.050

THE ROLE
Chelios might not have the numbers or provide the physicality that he did in his prime, but he's still a vital piece on the Wings. The oldest player in the NHL provides a needed veteran presence to a team with a lot of younger players who weren't around when the Wings made their last trip to the finals six years ago.

THE HONORS
Three-time Norris Trophy winner as NHL's top defenseman. Oldest player in the NHL.

DID YOU KNOW?
Owns Cheli's Chili Bar in Dearborn and Detroit.

QUOTABLE

"I don't really keep track of all the personal stuff. ... But that is something I would take a little pride in; if you look at my playoff games played, it's almost like three more years added on to my career."

CHRIS CHELIOS, Just before playing career playoff game No. 247, tying Patrick Roy for the all-time playoff record. Now, he's tops.

FAMILIAR FACE

Draper was 22 and single when he came to Detroit in 1993; he was 37 when he won his latest Cup, long married and has three children. "I've probably aged the worst," Draper said, laughing. "It's something that I'm really proud of. It just says that I've been on great teams with Detroit, been very fortunate to play with the players that I've played with. It's great."

HOCKEYTOWN HERO
KRIS DRAPER, CENTER

SPECIAL K
DRAPES A STAR IN FACE-OFF CIRCLE AND ON FORECHECK

ANDRE J. JACKSON

MERRY PRANKSTER
The inside scoop on Draper: Extremely fond of the letter "K"; has daughters Kennedi and Kamryn, and son Kienan. He decided the proximity of "J" to "K" would allow him to marry wife Julie. Called Braddock for likeness to "Col. Braddock" portrayer Chuck Norris. Has mastered the art of sneaking up on teammates celebrating birthdays and surprising them with a towel of shaving cream.

THE DRAPER FILE

THE BIO
AGE: 37
FROM: Toronto
HT/WT: 5-10, 188
EXPERIENCE: 17 years

STATS

GAMES ...65	PIM 68
GOALS 9	PP PTS 0
ASSISTS 8	SH PTS 2
POINTS ...17	SHOTS 97
+/- ....-2	SHOT % ...093

THE ROLE
Brings unmatched energy and hustle, and is an expert at taking face-offs and killing penalties.

HISTORY
■ Traded to Wings by Winnipeg for $1 on June 30, 1993.
■ Part owner of the International Hockey League's Flint Generals.

QUOTABLE
AFTER WINNING HIS FIRST STANLEY CUP:
"We knew it was big. I don't think anybody thought the parade was going to be like that."

HOCKEYTOWN HERO
VALTTERI FILPPULA, CENTER

FLIP FANTASTIC

FAST FINN
FINDS NICHE AS
SECOND LINER

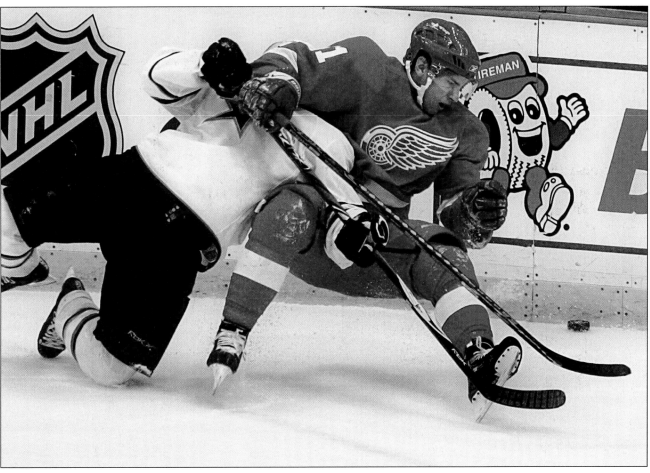

AMY LEANG

TRUE ICEMAN
Valtteri Filppula is from Finland, where there are many reindeer, especially in the northern part of the country. "We celebrate (Christmas) on the 24th of December," Filppula said. "First, we eat a big dinner. Then Santa comes to our place at night, around six or seven o'clock. We wait the whole day for him to show up." He said Finns believe Santa comes from Finland, not the North Pole.

THE FILPPULA FILE

BIO
AGE: 24
FROM: Vantaa, Finland
HT/WT: 6-0, 193
EXPERIENCE: 3 years

STATS

GAMES	...78	PIM	28
GOALS	19	PP PTS	8
ASSISTS	...17	SH PTS	0
POINTS	...36	SHOTS	...122
+/-	16	SHOT%	...156

ROLE
He's a mainstay on the No. 2 line and has scored some key goals in crucial spots in his young career.

HISTORY
■ Hockey idols as a youth were Teemu Selanne and Jari Kurri.
■ Only Finnish player to play for the Wings.

QUOTABLE
"The guys here make you feel so good. They get the tension away, so you can basically just concentrate on playing."

**DON'T MESS
WITH THE BIG MAN**
The story of Franzen's nickname, Mule: It was given to
him by former Wings captain
Steve Yzerman, because one
day Franzen, 6-feet-3 and 220
pounds, skated by and
Yzerman thought, "Wow, what
a mule." "He was just so big
and powerful," Yzerman said,
"and I just thought, 'That guy
is a mule.' "

KIRTHMON F. DOZIER

HOCKEYTOWN HERO
JOHAN FRANZEN, RIGHT WING

THE MULE

FROM GRINDER TO GOAL-SCORER, SWEDE IGNITES OFFENSE LATE IN SEASON

JULIAN H. GONZALEZ

BACK TO NATURE

Franzen, according to Niklas Kronwall, "sleeps a lot." But he's also well-informed and a lover of nature. "He's maybe the most intelligent person in here," Kronwall said. "I don't think he comes across like that a lot of times, but when you talk to him, you know that he knows his stuff. He likes to be out in nature. Back in Sweden, he'll take the bike out for a ride and come back with a bucket of blueberries."

THE FRANZEN FILE

BIO
AGE: 28
FROM: Vetlanda, Sweden
HT/WT: 6-3, 220
EXPERIENCE: 3 years

STATS

GAMES	...72	PIM	51
GOALS	27	PP PTS	16
ASSISTS	...11	SH PTS	1
POINTS	...38	SHOTS	...199
+/-	12	SHOT%	...136

ROLE
Franzen's offensive outburst not only etched his name in the club record books, it also took pressure off the first line.

HISTORY
■ Nicknamed Mule for his size and power.
■ Known among teammates as the go-to person when IKEA instructions need deciphering.

QUOTABLE
"When I get out there, I want to score, and I'm going to try to be in front of the net and get rebounds."

SMALL-TOWN STAR
Cleary is from Carbonear, Newfoundland. No player from the province of Newfoundland had won a Stanley Cup.

JULIAN H. GONZALEZ

HOCKEYTOWN HERO
DANIEL CLEARY, FORWARD

DAN THE MAN

BROKEN JAW SLOWED BUT DIDN'T STOP POWER FORWARD

JULIAN H. GONZALEZ

SEEING CLEAR-LY NOW

In January 1998, Cleary was arrested for drunken driving. He was 19. "I had money and a car, and I was living life to the fullest, but not the smartest," Cleary said. "It's almost as if you think you're invincible, I guess. It's sad to say that you need something like that to happen to you, to kind of wake you up, but that's what happened to me. I got pulled over. Nothing good could come out of that but to learn. And I believe these experiences have truly made me a better person."

THE CLEARY FILE

BIO

AGE: 29

FROM: Carbonear Newfoundland

HT/WT: 6-0, 210

EXPERIENCE: 10th season

STATS

GAMES	...63	PIM	33
GOALS	20	PP PTS	12
ASSISTS	...22	SH PTS	1
POINTS	...42	SHOTS	...177
+/-	21	SHOT%	...113

ROLE

A true power forward with an accurate shot, Cleary is a testament to the Wings' depth as he usually logs minutes on the third line.

HISTORY

■ 42 points in 2007-08 were a career high.
■ Missed chunk of season with broken jaw.
■ Favorite singer is Lenny Kravitz.

QUOTABLE

"He's got good hockey sense, he's strong on the puck. I think he's got a bright future."
— Mike Babcock

JULIAN H. GONZALEZ

HOME SWEET HOME

Holmstrom, on being with Detroit since 1996: "Why move when you like it so much here? I know my family is going to have it good here, and that's a big part of it, too. And I love, love to be on a winning team."

HOCKEYTOWN HERO
TOMAS HOLMSTROM, LEFT WING

HOMER

IT'S NOT ALWAYS PRETTY, BUT SWEDE GETS THE JOB DONE NEAR THE CREASE

MANDI WRIGHT

COMIC RELIEF
The inside scoop on Tomas Holmstrom: Masterfully mangles the English language as well as his native Swedish; often accused by teammates of being Finnish, or from the North Pole (quite possibly Santa Claus), and having the least-curved stick in hockey.

THE HOLMSTROM FILE

BIO
AGE: 35
FROM: Pieta, Sweden
HT/WT: 6-0, 203
EXPERIENCE: 10th season

Zetterberg

STATS			
		+/-	9
GAMES	...59	PIM	58
GOALS	20	PP PTS	18
ASSISTS	...20	SH PTS	0
POINTS	...40	SHOTS	...137

ROLE
Possibly most important member of the Wings' top line, he has received the admiration of his peers for his work in front of the net.

HISTORY
■ Three-time Stanley Cup winner.
■ Won a gold medal with Sweden at the 2006 Olympics.

QUOTABLE
"When they get the puck, you know something is going to happen all the time." — On linemates Pavel Datsyuk and Henrik

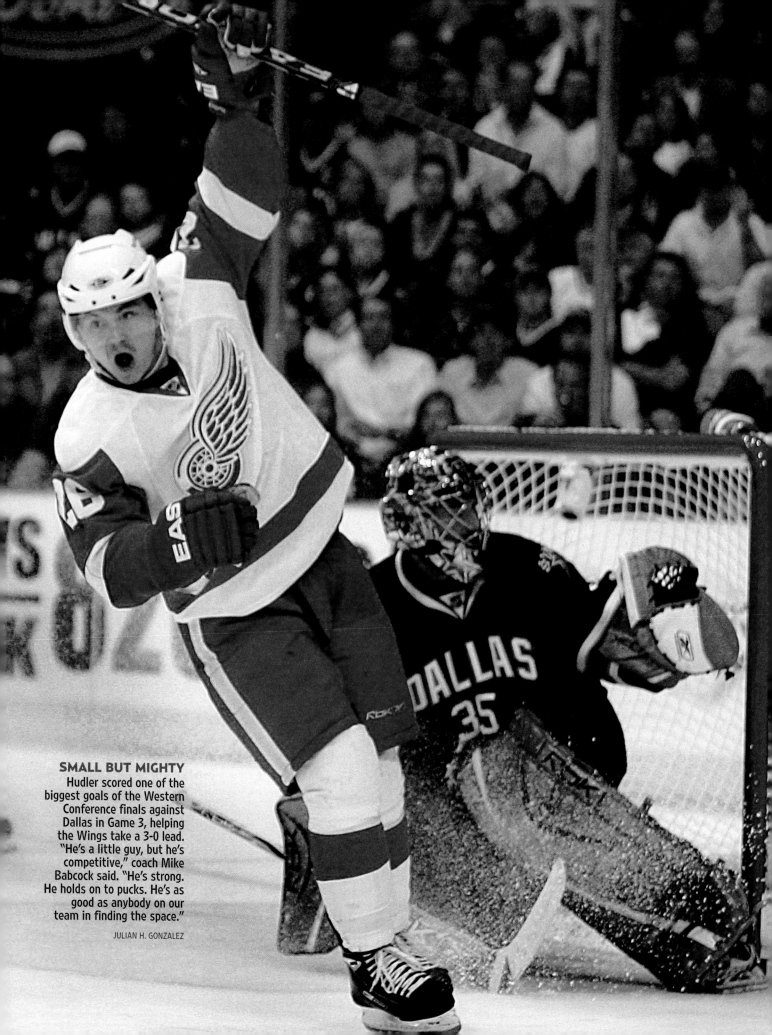

SMALL BUT MIGHTY
Hudler scored one of the biggest goals of the Western Conference finals against Dallas in Game 3, helping the Wings take a 3-0 lead. "He's a little guy, but he's competitive," coach Mike Babcock said. "He's strong. He holds on to pucks. He's as good as anybody on our team in finding the space."

JULIAN H. GONZALEZ

HOCKEYTOWN HERO
JIRI HUDLER, RIGHT WING

CZECH MATE

LITTLE HUDLER MAKES BIG PLAYS ON OFFENSE FOR WINGS

JULIAN H. GONZALEZ

EURO ROOTS
Here it is, an annual playoff tradition: the Red Wings' playing-soccer-in-the-hallway photo. Practice basically was called off one day, and Kris Draper, right, was foolish enough to take on a European guy — Jiri Hudler — in soccer.

THE HUDLER FILE

BIO

AGE: 24

FROM: Olomouc, Czechoslovakia

HT/WT: 5-9, 178

EXPERIENCE: 4th season

STATS

GAMES	...81	PIM	26
GOALS	13	PP PTS	15
ASSISTS	...29	SH PTS	 0
POINTS	...42	SHOTS	...131
+/-	11	SHOT%	...099

ROLE

A tough-yet-undersized backup forward with a tremendous shot, Hudler is another of the Wings' gifted offensive players.

HISTORY

■ Signed two-year, $2-million deal in July 2007.
■ 42 Points in 2007-08 were career high.
■ Played for the Czech pro team Vsetin at 15.

QUOTABLE

"He's got a great shot. He can shoot the puck hard for a smaller guy, and it's accurate."
— Chris Osgood

HOCKEYTOWN HERO
DARREN McCARTY, RIGHT WING

BIG MAC

FROM HARD ROCK TO HARD FALL TO HARD RETURN, GRINDER GIVES WINGS GRIT

KIRTHMON F. DOZIER

COMEBACK MAC

McCarty returned to the Wings in an amazing comeback. He was bankrupt from gambling and bad business deals. And he was out of hockey, released after the 2006-07 season by the Calgary Flames. The Flames had signed McCarty as a free agent after the Red Wings bought out his contract after the 2004-05 lockout.

THE McCARTY FILE

BIO

AGE: 36

FROM: Burnaby, British Columbia

HT/WT: 6-1, 210

EXPERIENCE: 14th season

STATS

GAMES	3	PIM	2
GOALS	0	PP PTS	0
ASSISTS	1	SH PTS	0
POINTS	1	SHOTS	3
+/-	2	SHOT%	...000

ROLE

A fan favorite, McCarty is one of six current Wings who has been around for three Stanley Cups.

HISTORY

■ Former lead singer for rock band Grinder.

■ Is a longtime professional wrestling fan.

■ Part of Grind Line with Draper and Maltby.

QUOTABLE

"Just to be back with this team, and making my way back and planning to be here as a supporting guy ... it's all a dream come true."

SAM I AM •
On the ice, Samuelsson is a big body who scored two goals in Game 1 of the Cup finals. Off the ice, he out-performed all his team-mates at a bowling tour-nament.

MANDI WRIGHT

HOCKEYTOWN HERO
MIKAEL SAMUELSSON, RIGHT WING

GRAND SAM

BIG SWEDE GETS
COMFORTABLE IN THE
PLAYOFF SPOTLIGHT

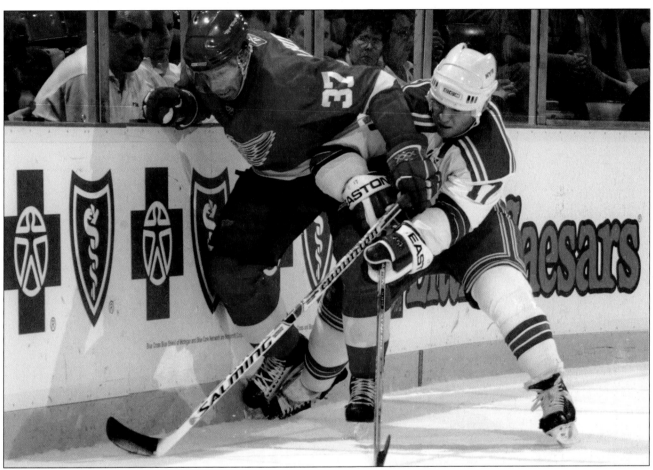

JULIAN H. GONZALEZ

TIES THAT BIND

Swedes Mikael Samuelsson and Andreas Lilja are close friends and usually drive to the rink together. In 2006, they looked for homes in Northville, Novi and surrounding communities. The Wings' other Swedes lived in that area, except Henrik Zetterberg, who lived in Birmingham. "Me and Lils looked at 60 or 70 houses," Samuelsson said. Their search ended when one found a house he liked. They then found a house that was similar, but not identical, about 100 feet away.

THE SAMUELSSON FILE

BIO
AGE: 31
FROM: Mariefred, Sweden
HT/WT: 6-2, 213
EXPERIENCE: 8th season

STATS

GAMES	...73	PIM	26
GOALS	11	PP PTS	11
ASSISTS	...29	SH PTS	0
POINTS	...40	SHOTS	...249
+/-	21	SHOT%	...044

ROLE
An imposing combination of size and speed, Samuelsson adds depth and scoring to the Wings' bench.

HISTORY
■ Traded three times in his NHL career.
■ His father, Christer Andersson, owns a canoe rental business in Sweden.

QUOTABLE
"He's a huge man; he's probably the biggest man on our team. You just look at him; he's as thick as they come."
— Mike Babcock

GET PHYSICAL
On the ice, Kronwall is a monster open-ice hitter who loves to pinch. Off the ice, he is accused by Dan Cleary of wearing pants entirely too tight; otherwise he's busy exchanging friendly barbs with Johan Franzen.

AMY LEANG

THE HITMAN

FINALLY HEALTHY, DEFENSEMAN PROVIDES BIG BOOMS ON SECOND DEFENSIVE PAIRING

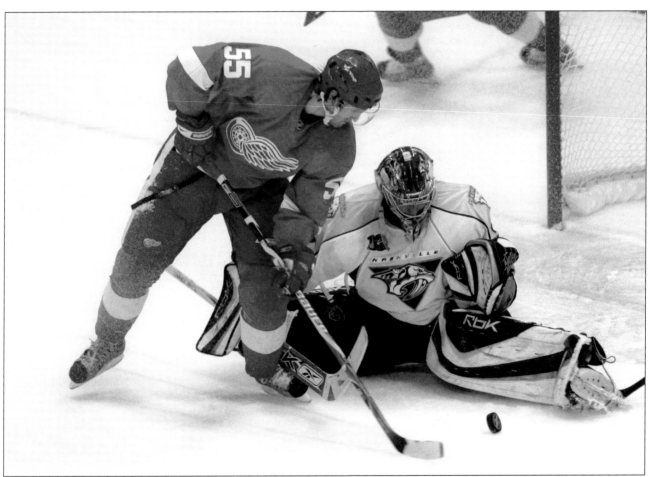

KIRTHMON F. DOZIER

BAD BREAKS

Niklas Kronwall's physicality is all the more amazing considering his history of fluky injuries. Kronwall suffered a broken leg during pregame warm-ups in 2003-04. He blew out a knee during an exhibition in September 2005. He had to wear a full cage for a while in 2006-07 when Avalanche forward Marek Svatos' skate nearly sliced off Kronwall's nose. And he missed the 2007 playoffs because of a fractured sacrum.

THE KRONWALL FILE

BIO

AGE: 27

FROM: Stockholm, Sweden

HT/WT: 6-0, 189

EXPERIENCE: 4th season

STATS

GAMES	... 65	PIM	 44
GOALS	 7	PP PTS	 8
ASSISTS	... 28	SH PTS	 0
POINTS	... 35	SHOTS	... 108
+/-	 25	SHOT%	...065

ROLE

Kronwall's big hits have turned heads at Joe Louis Arena, but he also has shown the ability to create offense with his solid passing.

HISTORY

■ Won gold medal with Sweden at 2006 Olympics.
■ Brother Staffan plays for the Toronto Maple Leafs.

QUOTABLE

"It's all about timing and balance — catch the guy at the right moment. You don't have to be 6-foot-7 and weigh 250."

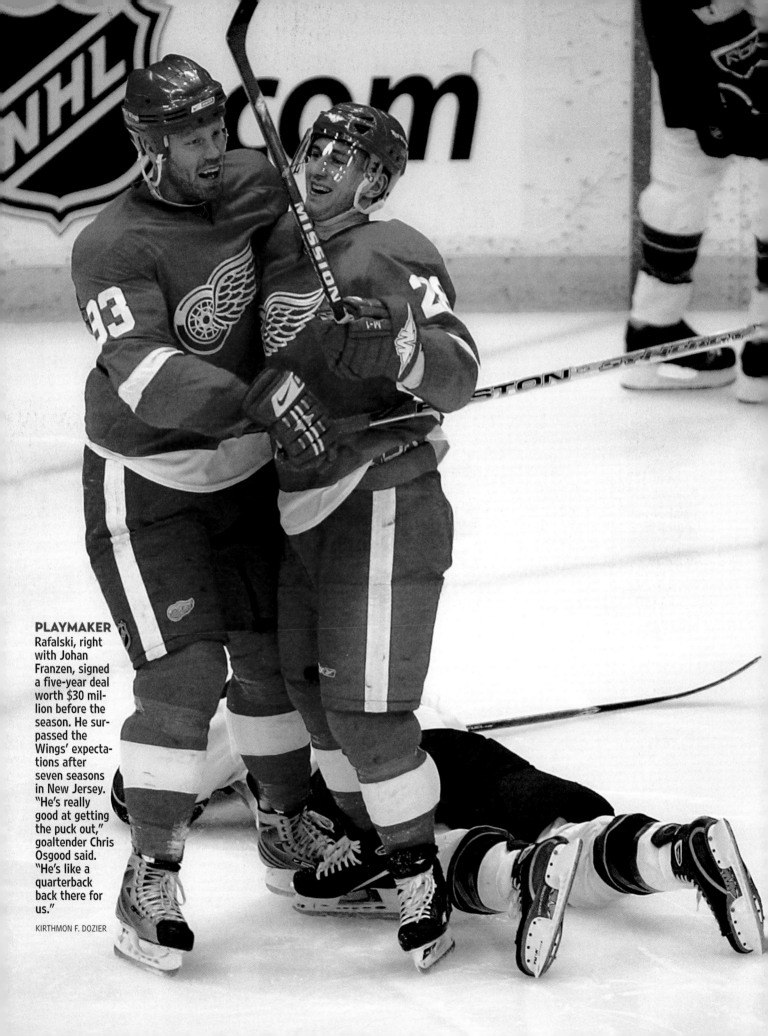

PLAYMAKER
Rafalski, right with Johan Franzen, signed a five-year deal worth $30 million before the season. He surpassed the Wings' expectations after seven seasons in New Jersey. "He's really good at getting the puck out," goaltender Chris Osgood said. "He's like a quarterback back there for us."

KIRTHMON F. DOZIER

HOCKEYTOWN HERO
BRIAN RAFALSKI, DEFENSEMAN

HOMETOWN BOY
DEARBORN NATIVE HAS OFFENSIVE SKILLS

JULIAN H. GONZALEZ

FROM THE D
Rafalski, right with Tomas Holmstrom, played youth hockey in the Detroit area, from about age 9 to 15. He shoots right and has played almost exclusively with Nicklas Lidstrom, who shoots left. It's a pairing that allows for fast passes on the power play and, if they switch sides, two powerful shots.

THE RAFALSKI FILE

BIO
AGE: 34
FROM: Dearborn
HT/WT: 5-10, 200
EXPERIENCE: 8th season

STATS
GAMES ... 73	PIM 34
GOALS 13	PP PTS 31
ASSISTS ...42	SH PTS 0
POINTS ...55	SHOTS ...175
+/- 27	SHOT% ...074

ROLE
Rafalski is a solid all-around defender whose mobility and smarts allow him to get to pucks and clear them out of the zone with ease.

HISTORY
■ Played five seasons in Europe.
■ Won two Cups with the New Jersey Devils.
■ Named to three All-Star teams.

QUOTABLE
"Coming home played a factor in my decision. We're very excited."
— Rafalski, on being near his family again.

TEAM SPIRIT
Hasek was relegated to back-up duty after subpar games in Round 1. But he was a great team guy and didn't sulk about not playing.

JULIAN H. GONZALEZ

DOMINATOR

GOALIE DOESN'T LET AGE SLOW HIM IN QUEST FOR SECOND CUP

JULIAN H. GONZALEZ

CULTURE CLUB
Dominik Hasek, on Easter in his native Czech Republic: Egg hunts are part of the holiday, but, "There's always Monday off at work. They stay home, and the family visits each other. Sunday's the holiday, and Monday's the day off. There is no special dinner. The special thing is every family has like a gingerbread lamb. It's made of gingerbread and on top is chocolate. After lunch or in the afternoon, everyone sits with cup of tea or coffee and they cut it and eat it."

THE HASEK FILE

BIO
AGE: 43
FROM: Pardubice, Czechoslovakia
HT/WT: 5-11, 177
EXPERIENCE: 16 years

STATS

GAMES ... 41	OTL 3
WINS 27	GAA 2.14
LOSSES ... 10	SV% 902

ROLE
Hasek was the primary starter for the Wings — and a good one at that — until he was benched for Game 5 of the first round against Nashville.

HISTORY
■ Led the Czech national team to the gold medal in the 1998 Winter Olympics.
■ Has own "Dominator" clothing line.

QUOTABLE
"Of course, it's disappointing for me to sit on the bench. ... But I understand the situation right now."

THE BENCH

FROM ABDELKADER TO QUINCEY, THESE PLAYERS FILLED A NEED FOR THE RED WINGS

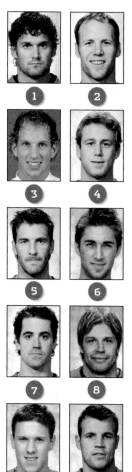

AMY LEANG

THE NAKED TOOTH

The Wings lost a few teeth on their way to the Cup. Darren McCarty sports the most well-known grin among current Wings. He said when he lost his right front tooth for the first time eight years ago, "my mom was devastated." He said he had a post and a replacement tooth put in, but the tooth kept getting knocked out when he played. Kirk Maltby figures he has broken his front teeth "10 to 15 times" over the years. And only about 50% of the Wings wear mouth guards, because some say they impair breathing.

① BRETT LEBDA
DEFENSEMAN

THE BIO

AGE: 26
FROM: Buffalo Grove, Ill.
HT/WT: 5-9, 195
EXP: Third season
DRAFTED: Undrafted
2008 SALARY: $550,000

THE ROLE

Lebda usually plays on the third line, using his speed and puck-handling abilities to compensate for his size.

THE HISTORY

Selected to the CCHA all-rookie team during his freshman year at Notre Dame.

THE STATS

GAMES .. 78	POINTS .. 14
GOALS 3	+/- ...... -1
ASSISTS .. 11	PIM...... 48

⑦ MARK HARTIGAN
CENTER

THE BIO

AGE: 30
FROM: Fort St. John, British Columbia
HT/WT: 6, 200
EXP: Sixth season
DRAFTED: Undrafted
2008 SALARY: $550,000

THE ROLE

Hartigan filled in for some of the Red Wings regulars when they were injured at the end of the season. Hartigan saw limited time on the Wings' fourth line.

THE HISTORY

A finalist for the 2002 Hobey Baker Award.

THE STATS

GAMES ...23	POINTS 4
GOALS 3	+/- ...... -2
ASSISTS ... 1	PIM...... 16

CONNECT THE WINGS: The lines the
Wings used most often in 2007-08:

	Datsyuk	Zetterberg	Franzen	Filppula	Deans Baals		
		Holmstrom		Samuelsson		Cleary	Maltby

2 KIRK MALTBY
LEFT WING

THE BIO

AGE: 35
FROM: Guelph, Ontario
HT/WT: 6-0, 193
EXP: 15th season
DRAFTED: By Edmonton, 1992, Round 3, No. 65 overall
2008 SALARY: $950,000

THE ROLE

Grind Line vet is a penalty-killing specialist who's good in his zone and has been known to score a goal.

THE HISTORY

Scored an NHL career-best 37 points in 2002-03 with the Wings.

THE STATS

GAMES ... 61	POINTS ... 10
GOALS 6	+/- ...... -8
ASSISTS ... 4	PIM 32

3 JUSTIN ABDELKADER
LEFT WING

THE BIO

AGE: 21
FROM: Muskegon
HT/WT: 6-2, 203
EXP: Rookie
DRAFTED: By Red Wings, 2005, Round 2, No. 42 overall
2008 SALARY: N/A

THE ROLE

Left wing from MSU played in two games, then made the playoff roster for depth. He is an excellent skater with good defense.

THE HISTORY

Won 2004 Mr. Hockey Award in Michigan.

THE STATS

GAMES 2	POINTS 0
GOALS 0	+/- 0
ASSISTS ... 0	PIM 2

4 DEREK MEECH
DEFENSEMAN

THE BIO

AGE: 24
FROM: Winnipeg, Manitoba
HT/WT: 5-11, 197
EXP: Second season
DRAFTED: By Red Wings, 2002, Round 7, No. 229 overall
2008 SALARY: N/A

THE ROLE

Stepped in this season when some other Wings suffered injuries. Meech likely will see more time next season.

THE HISTORY

Favorite player growing up was Wayne Gretzky.

THE STATS

GAMES ... 32	POINTS 3
GOALS 0	+/-....... -5
ASSISTS ... 3	PIM 6

5 ANDREAS LILJA
DEFENSEMAN

THE BIO

AGE: 32
FROM: Helsin, Sweden
HT/WT: 6-3, 220
EXP: Eighth season
DRAFTED: By Los Angeles, 2000, Round 2, No. 54 overall
2008 SALARY: $1 mil.

THE ROLE

Stay-at-home defenseman was solid and is known for reliability in his zone and his willingness to block shots, especially on penalties.

THE HISTORY

Enjoys playing hearts on trips to away games.

THE STATS

GAMES ... 79	POINTS ...12
GOALS 2	+/- .... -2
ASSISTS .. 10	PIM 93

6 KYLE QUINCEY
DEFENSEMAN

THE BIO

AGE: 22
FROM: Kitchener, Ontario
HT/WT: 6-2, 207
EXP: Third season
DRAFTED: By Red Wings, 2003, Round 4, No. 132 overall
2008 SALARY: N/A

THE ROLE

In only a handful of games, his style of play has been compared to Chris Chelios.

THE HISTORY

Born during Chelios' third NHL season.

THE STATS

GAMES 6	POINTS 0
GOALS 0	+/- ...... -3
ASSISTS ... 0	PIM 4

8 BRAD STUART
DEFENSEMAN

THE BIO

AGE: 28
FROM: Rocky Mountain House, Alberta
HT/WT: 6-2, 213
EXP: Eighth season
DRAFTED: By San Jose, 1998, Round 1, No. 3 overall
2008 SALARY: $3,500,000

THE ROLE

A top-four defenseman since arriving from L.A. at the deadline.

THE HISTORY

Played for four teams (BOS, CGY, LA, DET) the past two seasons.

THE STATS

GAMES 9	POINTS 2
GOALS 1	+/- 6
ASSISTS ... 1	PIM 2

9 JIMMY HOWARD
GOALIE

THE BIO

AGE: 24
FROM: Syracuse, N.Y.
HT/WT: 6-0, 205
EXP: Second season
DRAFTED: By Red Wings, 2003, Round 2, No. 64 overall
2008 SALARY: N/A

THE ROLE

Played most of the season in Grand Rapids; projects as goalie of the future. Called up when Hasek was injured.

THE HISTORY

Named USA Hockey goaltender of the year in 2002.

THE STATS

GAMES 4	OTL 0
WINS 0	GAA 2.13
LOSSES ... 2	SV% .... .926

10 AARON DOWNEY
RIGHT WING

THE BIO

AGE: 33
FROM: Shelburne, Ontario
HT/WT: 6-1, 215
EXP: 8th season
DRAFTED: Undrafted
2008 SALARY: N/A

THE ROLE

Downey is the enforcer. Downey sticks up for teammates and adds toughness to a team known more for skill than grit.

THE HISTORY

Says hardest he's ever been hit was by the Flames' Robyn Regehr.

THE STATS

GAMES ... 56	POINTS 3
GOALS 0	+/- 0
ASSISTS ... 3	PIM 116

11 DALLAS DRAKE
RIGHT WING

THE BIO

AGE: 39
FROM: Trail, British Columbia
HT/WT: 6-0, 186
EXP: 15th season
DRAFTED: 1989 Round 6 Pick 116, Red Wings
2008 SALARY: $550,000

THE ROLE

A tough fourth-liner who knows his role and mixes it up well, a good penalty-killer and leader.

THE HISTORY

Won 1991 NCAA hockey title at Northern Michigan in junior year.

THE STATS

GAMES ... 65	POINTS 6
GOALS 3	+/- ...... -12
ASSISTS ... 3	PIM 41

12 DARREN HELM
CENTER

THE BIO

AGE: 21
FROM: Winnipeg, Manitoba
HT/WT: 5-11, 172
EXP: 1st year
DRAFTED: 2005 Round 5 Pick 132, Red Wings
2008 SALARY: N/A

THE ROLE

A checking forward who fit in nicely on the fourth line. He's a quick skater with soft hands and plays bigger than his size.

THE HISTORY

Played for Canada in the '07 Junior Worlds.

THE STATS

GAMES 7	POINTS 0
GOALS 0	+/- ...... -2
ASSISTS ... 0	PIM 2

THE PLAYOFFS

The Wings entered the 2008 playoffs with the outside expectations laden on a team that finished with the best record in the regular season, and with the internal memory of how close they came to realizing those same expectations in 2007.

But it was a better Detroit team that embarked on the playoffs this time, thanks to a newly acquired Brad Stuart, a healthy Niklas Kronwall and a reinvented Chris Osgood. Better because, "we're the deepest team in the playoffs," Osgood said.

"To win you need a little bit of everything," captain Nicklas Lidstrom said. "You're going to have your bumps and bruises throughout a long playoff run, so you need to have good depth, and I think we have that. ... And you need to be a little lucky, too."

PLAYOFF EXCITEMENT

The spotlight was back on Detroit and Joe Louis Arena for the playoffs. The fans were pumped. The octopi were ready. And the Red Wings didn't disappoint.

BRIAN KAUFMAN

ROUND 1, GAME 1
RED WINGS 3, PREDATORS 1

Z-LIGHTFUL

ZETTERBERG, STARS BREAK STALEMATE WITH BIG 3RD PERIOD

WINGS LEAD SERIES, 1-0

HERO
HENRIK ZETTERBERG
Zetterberg scored the winning goal and added an empty-netter for insurance late in the third period.

GOATS
THE TOP PREDATORS
The Preds got zip from top scorers J.P. Dumont (two SOG, minus-3) and Jason Arnott (no SOG, minus-1).

COUNT 'EM!

15

Wins for the Wings' 11th Stanley Cup.

BIG STAT
Chris Chelios played his 247th playoff game, an NHL record.

WINGIN' IT
Jordin Tootoo scored for the Predators, minutes after he'd had a stare-down contest with Darren McCarty.

QUOTABLE
"You want to try to intimidate each other. We all know what he brings to the game, and they all know what I bring to the game. I'm not going to back down."
JORDIN TOOTOO, on McCarty.

TWO CENTS
MITCH ALBOM
If the Wings have learned one other playoff lesson the hard way — besides not turning goaltenders from "Joe Who?" into "Joe Wow!" — it's this: Your stars have to score. Zetterberg is the Red Wings' star, their heir apparent to the Steve Yzerman mantle. Getting two goals in the playoff opener immediately relaxes him and makes the other team worry.

LONG GONE
Nashville goaltender Dan Ellis looks back into the net as Johan Franzen's shot crosses the line for a goal early in Game 1. The tally was the first of many for Franzen and the Wings in their '08 playoff run.

JULIAN H. GONZALEZ

DISCO DEMOLITION

Tomas Holmstrom celebrates as the puck bounces out of the net after blocking the sight of goalie Dan Ellis on a goal by teammate Nicklas Lidstrom. Holmstrom's pestering in front of the net was key to the Wings' offense all season and a source of controversy later in the playoffs.

KIRTHMON F. DOZIER

ROUND 1, GAME 2
WINGS 4, PREDATORS 2

LIKE OLD TIMES
WINGS GET A VETERAN GOAL RUSH

WINGS LEAD SERIES, 2-0

COUNT 'EM!

14

Wins for the Wings' 11th Stanley Cup.

HERO
DARREN MCCARTY
His goal just 2:26 into the first period capped an improbable return to the lineup and gave Wings fans chills.

GOATS
PREDS' TOP LINE
Jason Arnott, J.P. Dumont and Jan Hlavac took more penalties (three) than shots (two) and were again held off the score sheet.

BIG STAT
It took just 11 seconds in the second period for the Predators to erase their 2-0 deficit.

WINGIN' IT
McCarty's goal was his first as a Wing in more than four years and his first as a Wing in the playoffs in nearly six years.

TWO CENTS WORTH
MITCH ALBOM
Chelios, Draper, Lidstrom, McCarty and Holmstrom — who scored Game 2's last goal — were on the team that won the Wings' last Cup in 2002. But the other guys never left. McCarty has been to hell and back. Divorced, in rehab, in debt, in denial. To see him sweating by his locker again, a bandaged cut above his right eye, is to believe that not every sad story is helpless.

QUOTABLE

"He's worked for everything. To think of how far he's come since (then) to now scoring an NHL playoff goal ... everybody in this state is happy for him."

KRIS DRAPER, on McCarty.

ROUND 1, GAME 3
PREDATORS 5, RED WINGS 3

PRED ALERT

NASHVILLE STORMS BACK AT HOME WITH RAPID-FIRE GOALS

WINGS LEAD SERIES, 2-1

HERO
JASON ARNOTT
The Predators captain emerged from a series-long funk by slapping in the winning goal in the third period.

GOAT
DOMINIK HASEK
The Wings goalie is suddenly giving up goals in pairs: Two quick ones in the second period of Game 2, two quick ones in the second period Game 3, and then the dagger — two goals in nine seconds near the end of the third.

BIG STAT
Grosse Pointe Woods' David Legwand — making his first appearance of the series — scored Nashville's second goal and was the game's only player to finish at plus-3.

QUOTABLE
"I know I could make a save, but it's not easy. He's skating fast, he's in the middle of the ice, and he had time to prepare for the shot. It goes probably 98 miles per hour, and he hit the top corner."
DOMINIK HASEK, on Arnott.

COUNT 'EM!
14
Wins for the Wings' 11th Stanley Cup.

WINGIN' IT
Jiri Hudler's second-period goal, which gave the Wings a 2-0 lead, was his first career playoff goal.

TWO CENTS WORTH
MICHAEL ROSENBERG
You still have to like the Red Wings in this series. Yes, I know: The Wings have experience with the early-round collapse. They are close personal friends with the early-round collapse. But this just doesn't have that feel.

WINGS WORRY
JULIAN H. GONZALEZ
Nashville captain Jason Arnott celebrates his team's first goal. Arnott's goal cut the Wings' lead to 2-1 and began a three-period hot streak that would stretch into Game 4 and eventually spell disaster for Dominik Hasek.

KEY CHANGE

JULIAN H. GONZALEZ

Kris Draper watches as backup goalie Chris Osgood comes in for starter Dominik Hasek after Hasek gave up his third unanswered goal. The change came too late for the Wings to turn around Game 4, but it marked the turning point in the Wings' '08 playoff run.

ROUND 1, GAME 4
PREDATORS 3, RED WINGS 2

ROADBLOCKS

QUICK GOALS AGAIN ARE WINGS' UNDOING

SERIES TIED, 2-2

COUNT 'EM!

14

Wins for the Wings' 11th Stanley Cup.

QUOTABLE

"Puck went in. The puck's going in the net. And that can't be the case."

MIKE BABCOCK, on why he pulled Hasek.

HERO
DAN ELLIS
Give the kid credit. Not only did he outplay the Dominator, but he was able to hold off the swarming Red Wings.

GOATS
DOMINIK HASEK
Giving up goals in bunches, at the worst times — not a good combination. "Worst hockey I've played in my life."

BIG STAT
32: Seconds that ticked off the clock between Nashville's first-period goals, which gave the Predators a 2-0 lead.

TWO CENTS WORTH
MICHAEL ROSENBERG
This is not an easy decision. If Babcock goes with Osgood, he probably has to stick with him for the rest of the series and beyond. He can't go back and forth. But if Babcock gives Hasek one more chance, and Hasek plays the way he did the past two games, the Wings likely will find themselves on the brink of elimination.

WINGIN' IT
Chris Osgood stopped all 13 shots he faced in relief of Hasek, showing that the Wings have a better bullpen than the Tigers.

NOT THE DOMINATOR

JULIAN H. GONZALEZ

Vernon Fiddler celebrates Jordin Tootoo's goal in Game 2 on Dominik Hasek. In Game 4, Nashville became the first team to go from trailing to leading in under 10 seconds by scoring two goals within nine seconds. Hasek was replaced by Chris Osgood for Game 5.

CZECHING IN & OUT

GOALIE SWITCH WAS FRAUGHT WITH RISK AND REWARD

BY DREW SHARP AND MICHAEL ROSENBERG

Red Wings coach Mike Babcock opted for pulling the panic alarm when he pulled the plug on goalie Dominik Hasek.

Babcock justified his decision to start Chris Osgood in Game 5 as a continuation of a successful regular-season rotation.

But in the playoffs, you ride a guy until he tosses you into the abyss.

Babcock made a move to win a series, believing Osgood represented the better chance of beating the gritty Predators.

He probably lost Hasek for good with this decision.

"The puck didn't hit him in Nashville," Babcock said. "The bottom line is we've done this all year long. Ozzie has been very, very good for us. I thought Ozzie played well (in Game 4), so that's what we're doing."

Hasek knew the odds of his benching were good after surrendering soft goals in consecutive games.

"It's Ozzie's time to step up," Hasek said. "Ozzie is No. 1 guy. It's disappointing, but it's the way it is. The coaches believe they made the best decision."

Osgood enjoyed a career renaissance this season: Starting for the West in the All-Star Game, receiving a three-year contract extension and winning the Cup.

Osgood was forced to raise his performance to a higher level than 1998.

How bad were Hasek's two games in

Nashville? He gave up three goals on 14 shots in Game 4, then went to the bench to watch the rest of the 3-2 loss.

The Wings have picked Hasek over Osgood three times: before the 2001-02 season, when they traded for Hasek; before last season, when they signed Hasek to be their No. 1 goalie even though Osgood already was on the roster; and then for this year's playoffs.

Hasek is 43, and because playing goalie is largely about reflexes, it's amazing he has lasted this long. Osgood is 35 and just finished the best regular season of his career.

After Hasek was pulled in Game 4, Osgood made big saves. Still, the switch wasn't an easy decision. Babcock knew that if he started Osgood in Game 5, he had to stick with him for the rest of the playoffs. He couldn't go back and forth.

The hunch worked.

TRUE DEFENDERS

Goalie Chris Osgood and teammates celebrate the Red Wings' 2-1 overtime win. Osgood didn't even reach half of opposing netminder Dan Ellis' 52 saves, but a staunch defense in front of him made his first playoff start of the season a successful one.

JULIAN H. GONZALEZ

ROUND 1, GAME 5
WINGS 2, PREDATORS 1 (OT)

FRAN-TASTIC MULE SCORES ON BREAKAWAY IN OT

WINGS LEAD SERIES, 3-2

COUNT 'EM!

13

Wins for the Wings' 11th Stanley Cup.

HERO
JOHAN FRANZEN
The Wing's sliding backhand won it in OT. "Just a turnover in the neutral zone, something they feast on," Preds goalie Dan Ellis said.

GOAT
RYAN SUTER
Preds defenseman turned over the puck to Franzen. "We wasted that good goaltending effort," Nashville coach Barry Trotz said of Ellis' 52 saves.

BIG STAT
Nicklas Lidstrom's 197th playoff game broke Steve Yzerman's team record.

WINGIN' IT
The Wings were told by the NHL that octopus wrangler Al Sobotka could no longer swing the mollusks over his head while removing them from the ice at the Joe. If he (or anyone else) did, the team would be fined $10,000. That's $1,250 per tentacle.

QUOTABLE

"(J.P.) Dumont tried to put it out to their D-man and it ended up right on my blade, almost. I just saw Mule in the corner of my eye and tried to give it to him. It wasn't really a good pass — he was just able to handle it really well and he came in and scored."

NIKLAS KRONWALL, on Franzen's winner.

TWO CENTS WORTH
MITCH ALBOM
Thank goodness this guy isn't as stubborn as his nickname, Mule, or we might still be at Joe Louis Arena, waiting for a score. Or worse. We'd be shaking our heads wondering why anyone bothers to play the regular season in the NHL. Honestly, until Franzen's game-winner, which exhaled Detroit to a 3-2 lead in this first-round series, this night was like trying to stuff a fistful of pennies into a piggy bank. You may have riches all over your lap, but you have precious little in the place where you need it.

ROUND 1, GAME 6
WINGS 3, PREDATORS 0

SKIP AHEAD
CAPTAIN'S LONG SHOT, OZZIE'S SHUTOUT SEND WINGS TO ROUND 2

WINGS WIN SERIES, 4-2

JULIAN H. GONZALEZ

FROM SHAKY TO SHUTOUT
Goalie Chris Osgood makes a save as the Predators' J.P. Dumont skates in during the second period. Osgood's 11th career playoff shutout was enough to guide the Wings to their first road win of the playoffs.

COUNT 'EM!

12

Wins for the Wings' 11th Stanley Cup.

HERO
CHRIS OSGOOD
He has taken the Red Wings from shaky to shutout goaltending. Overall, he gave up just one goal in 154 minutes against Nashville.

GOAT
ALEXANDER RADULOV
Not only was he a minus-2, he caused the already-under-manned Predators to miss Jason Arnott the past two games because of a goal-celebration concussion.

BIG STAT
This was the fourth consecutive season in which the Predators have lost in the first round.

WINGIN' IT
Nicklas Lidstrom's shot from the neutral zone that skipped past Dan Ellis evoked memories of the Wings' last Cup run in 2002. Trailing, 2-0, in the first round to Vancouver, Lidstrom scored from center ice on Dan Cloutier, jump-starting the Wings to win the next four games, then the Stanley Cup.

QUOTABLE
"I had no idea that you had to carry the losses of the franchise around with you everywhere you went after the playoffs."
MIKE BABCOCK, on avoiding an upset by Nashville.

TWO CENTS WORTH
DREW SHARP
It's safe now for everybody to open their eyes and put away the oxygen masks. The Wings got out of the first round without a headstone marking the premature demise of another promising championship run.

ALL GOOD

WINGS FEND OFF RIVALS, BARELY

WINGS LEAD SERIES, 1-0

HERO
JOHAN FRANZEN
The big Swede scored late in the first period to make it 3-1, then chased Jose Theodore with his second goal of the game early in the second period.

GOAT
JOSE THEODORE
The Avalanche goalie stopped only 12 of 16 shots and left with his team in a 4-1 hole early in the second period before getting pulled.

COUNT 'EM!
11
Wins for the Wings' 11th Stanley Cup.

BIG STAT
There were eight seconds left when Chris Osgood robbed ex-Spartan John-Michael Liles to preserve the victory.

WINGIN' IT
Franzen's three previous two-goal games were all in a 20-day span in March. "It's tough to take him down," Henrik Zetterberg said. "He's a big guy, and he's really strong on his skates. ... He makes the right plays out there, so it's really fun to see him scoring some goals."

QUOTABLE
"When they switched the goaltenders, I thought their team responded well. This time of year, nobody goes away. You really have to keep your foot on the pedal, keep putting them down."

DAN CLEARY, on being up 4-1 before hanging on for a one-goal win.

TWO CENTS WORTH
MITCH ALBOM
We wanted it to be special. We wanted it to be nostalgic — the old Avs versus the old Wings. But time marches on. Claude Lemieux retires. Steve Yzerman wears a suit. A team can get fined for slinging fish. Still, the Red Wings have long been about offensive skill, and scoring four goals in the first 22 minutes was a welcome flashback. On the other hand, almost blowing a 4-1 lead is not.

GOALIE CHASERS
The Wings celebrate Henrik Zetterberg's first-period goal. They stumbled late, but their hot start was enough to force goalie Jose Theodore to the bench.

JULIAN H. GONZALEZ

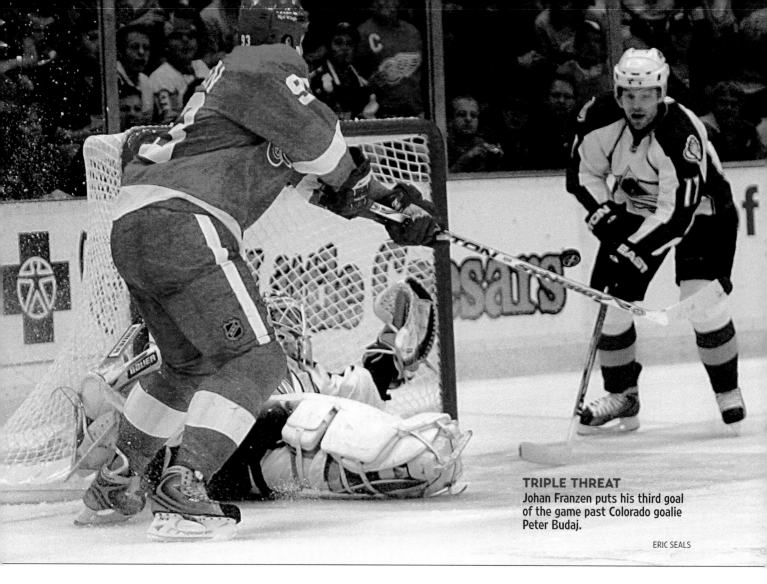

TRIPLE THREAT
Johan Franzen puts his third goal of the game past Colorado goalie Peter Budaj.

ERIC SEALS

ROUND 2, GAME 2
RED WINGS 5, AVALANCHE 1

HATS OFF

FRANZEN NETS 3; WINGS IN CONTROL

WINGS LEAD SERIES, 2-0

COUNT 'EM!

10

Wins for the 11th Cup.

HERO
JOHAN FRANZEN
The Mule continued his torrid pace, topping his Game 1 output — two goals — with a hat trick as the Red Wings romped to a 2-0 series lead.

GOAT
ALL OF THEM
Goalie Jose Theodore was chased for the second straight game, but the Avs were outshot, out-played, outfought and just plain overmatched.

BIG STAT
Goalie Jose Theodore allowed eight goals on just 36 shots through two games.

WINGIN' IT
It was the Wings' first playoff hat trick since Darren McCarty's on May 18, 2002, in the Western finals against ... the Avs.

QUOTABLE
"We gotta find ways to get a break in this series, whatever it is."
RYAN SMYTH, Colorado forward on falling behind 2-0 to the Wings.

TWO CENTS WORTH
DREW SHARP
Everyone must resist the urge to immediately take a shovel to the Avalanche's chances of making this an interesting series. The Avs are beaten down physically and mentally. But wasn't Nashville as well in the previous series?

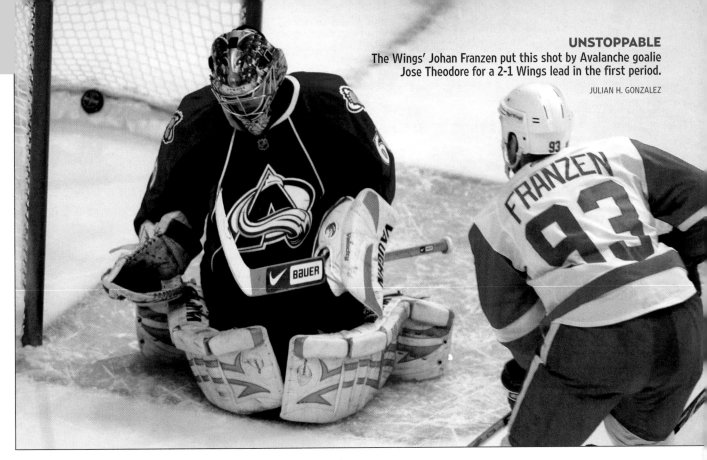

UNSTOPPABLE
The Wings' Johan Franzen put this shot by Avalanche goalie Jose Theodore for a 2-1 Wings lead in the first period.

JULIAN H. GONZALEZ

ROUND 2, GAME 3
RED WINGS 4, AVALANCHE 3

AVS NO RIVAL

DATSYUK, ZETTERBERG PUT COLORADO ON THE BRINK

WINGS LEAD SERIES, 3-0

COUNT 'EM!

9

Wins for the Wings' 11th Stanley Cup.

HERO
PAVEL DATSYUK
Two goals on three shots, an assist — it's great to see a star taking some of the scoring burden off Johan Franzen.

GOAT
PETER FORSBERG
He gave the Avs life, but his ill-timed double-minor gave the Wings a fourth goal Colorado couldn't overcome.

BIG STAT
Only two teams in NHL history have rallied from a 3-0 deficit to win a series — the '42 Maple Leafs (against the Wings) and the '75 Islanders.

WINGIN' IT
Peter Forsberg made his belated presence felt with some Swede-on-Swede violence, when he whacked Mikael Samuelsson in the chops with his stick. "Here comes Johan Franzen saying, 'Why are you doing that to a fellow countryman, you idiot?' " Mickey Redmond said on FSN. "So a little frustration at the Swedish contingent on the road team from the Swedish contingent on the home team." Ken Daniels said: "Well, they got their gold medal. Now all bets are off."

QUOTABLE
"Don't listen to anyone. You can't let yourself take it all too seriously."

JOHAN FRANZEN, on being praised after his Round 2 scores.

TWO CENTS WORTH
DREW SHARP
Perhaps the Avs' biggest problem is that the rivalry — or perhaps the rivalry that once was — means more to the Avalanche than it does to the Wings. The Avs wanted a fight, but it's obvious now that there's little fight left in this series.

ROUND 2, GAME 4
RED WINGS 8, AVALANCHE 2

SWEDE SWEEP

FRANZEN'S RECORD NIGHT SEALS THE DEAL

WINGS WIN SERIES, 4-0

COUNT 'EM!

8

Wins for the Wings' 11th Stanley Cup.

HERO
JOHAN FRANZEN
His second hat trick gave him nine goals for the series, breaking Gordie Howe's franchise record (eight in a seven-game series in 1949).

GOAT
AVS GOALIES
Jose Theodore got chased again (what's new?), and backup Peter Budaj allowed five goals in relief. Now they know how Patrick Roy used to feel.

BIG STAT
Franzen scored nine goals in the series, as many as the Avs.

WINGIN' IT
Franzen needed only 10 playoff games to score 11 goals and break the Red Wings' record for goals in one post-season, which was held by three players, including Brett Hull, who needed 23 games in 2002.

QUOTABLE
"Nothing's taken for granted. That's why you have to keep the pressure on and keep bringing it."
KRIS DRAPER, on the Wings' dominant performance in Game 4.

TWO CENTS WORTH
HELENE ST. JAMES
The Red Wings, in short, produced goals every which way: rushing the net, firing from the blue line, on power plays and shorthanded; utterly, completely and sweepingly ending their Western Conference semifinal against the Colorado Avalanche.

JOHANDY
Johan Franzen celebrates his third goal of the game, a power-play marker that gave the Wings a 7-1 lead late in the second period. The goal capped an incredible series for Franzen -- he scored nine goals in four games, equaling the total Colorado scored as a team. He set the Wings' record for goals in a postseason in just 10 games.

JULIAN H. GONZALEZ

ROUND 3, GAME 1
WINGS 4, STARS 1

POWERED UP

WINGS' SPECIAL TEAMS SHINE IN WESTERN FINALS OPENER

WINGS LEAD SERIES, 1-0

HERO
NIKLAS KRONWALL
He had two assists and got a standing ovation for leveling Antti Miettinen, driving into the hit with his left shoulder.

GOAT
MARTY TURCO
The ex-Wolverines goalie was tormented all night by Johan Franzen and Tomas Holmstrom in front of the net.

COUNT 'EM
7
Wins for the Wings' 11th Stanley Cup.

BIG STAT
Franzen scored in his fifth straight game, tying a franchise record.

WINGIN' IT
That Turco remained winless after the game at Joe Louis Arena in his eight-year NHL career was especially interesting considering he made himself at home with an 18-5 record at the Joe during his standout four-year career at Michigan.

QUOTABLE
"He just drives into people. It's great to see. People forget how much we missed him last year and how good of a player he is."

CHRIS OSGOOD, on Kronwall.

TWO CENTS WORTH
MITCH ALBOM
Niklas Kronwall plowed into his Dallas opponent like a football linebacker running to make a bus. Shoulder in. Opponent goes up. Opponent crashes. Kronwall skates away.

SCREEN STAR
Stars goalie Marty Turco wasn't happy that Tomas Holmstrom screened and aggravated him in a Game 1 win. "He's one of the best at it," Turco said. "He doesn't get enough credit probably for his hands, but he's certainly willing to pay the price and he's good and he got rewarded for it."

AMY LEANG

SLASH AND BURN

STARS' RIBEIRO DROPS OZZIE WITH LATE HIT

WINGS LEAD SERIES, 2-0

COUNT 'EM

6

Wins for the Wings' 11th Stanley Cup

BIG STAT

The last two-plus periods were scoreless. Henrik Zetterberg's goal at 15:13 of the first was the game-winner.

HERO

CHRIS OSGOOD
With leading scorer Johan Franzen sidelined, the Wings needed Osgood and he came through, stopping 17 shots and improving to 8-0 in the playoffs.

GOAT

MIKE RIBEIRO
Ribeiro became Public Enemy No. 1 in Hockeytown after dropping Ozzie with a two-handed slash to the chest as the game ended. "That's totally uncalled for," Wings captain Nicklas Lidstrom said. "He two-handed Ozzie right in the chest. I think he should be suspended for doing something like that."

WINGIN' IT
The Wings' record for consecutive playoff wins is 11, over the 1998 and 1999 playoffs.

QUOTABLE

"Something like that, that's right out of 'Slap Shot.' It was intended to injure our best player. Couldn't believe it when he did it." KRIS DRAPER, on Ribeiro's two-handed slash of Osgood

CHOKE 'EM
Detroit's Kris Draper controls Dallas' Mike Ribeiro, who took a stick to Chris Osgood's chest. Minutes before the Ribeiro incident, Draper took a punch to the head from Steve Ott. "I wasn't sure what he was thinking," Draper said of Ribeiro. "It's an intense series, there's a lot on the line, but that's just crossing the line. He swung from behind the net, a two-hander, right at Ozzie."

MANDI WRIGHT

TWO CENTS WORTH
MICHAEL ROSENBERG
It was bizarre, at the end, looking up and seeing that the final was only 2-1. But for the best indication of the Wings' dominance, you didn't need to look at the scoreboard. You had to look on the ice, where Ribeiro took out two nights' worth of frustration on Osgood's chest.

R O U N D   3 ,   G A M E   3
WINGS 5, STARS 2

UNSTOPPABLE

DATSYUK'S HAT TRICK PUTS STARS ON BRINK

WINGS LEAD SERIES, 3-0

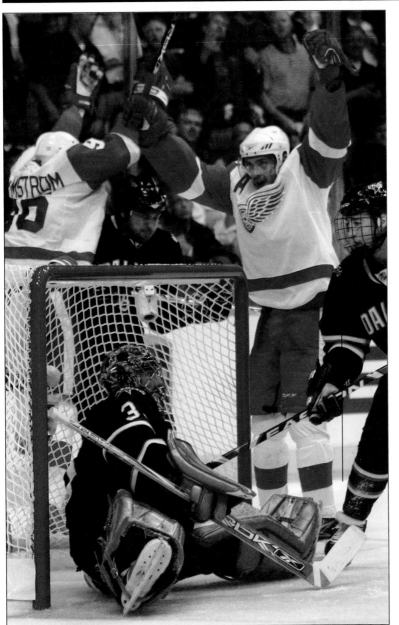

THREE-OH!
Tomas Holmstrom and Pavel Datsyuk celebrate one of Datsyuk's three goals. "That's one of his better games I've seen," Nicklas Lidstrom said of Datsyuk. The win was the Wings' ninth straight in the playoffs.

JULIAN H. GONZALEZ

HERO
PAVEL DATSYUK
He had a hat trick — on four shots — and a plus-four rating. This one wasn't really a tough choice, was it?

GOAT
MARTY TURCO
Five goals on 21 shots — after giving up five or more only twice earlier this season. Not the game he needed.

WINGIN' IT
Datsyuk's hat trick was his first in 73 playoff games and 518 total NHL games. "It looks like he's going to lose the puck, or someone is going to hit him, but somehow, he finds a way to keep control of the puck," Nicklas Lidstrom said.

COUNT 'EM!
5
Wins for the Wings' 11th Stanley Cup

BIG STAT
The Stars' power play was barely a flicker this series, going 1-for-15.

QUOTABLE
"We feel like we're not done yet. We have to get that fourth win. They're playing at home, they're going to come out and be a desperate team."
NICKLAS LIDSTROM

TWO CENTS WORTH
MICHAEL ROSENBERG
Even when Dallas was on the power play, the Wings had the puck all the time. When Wings forward Tomas Holmstrom went to the penalty box 18 seconds into the third period and the arena came to life, Zetterberg scored his shorthanded goal. That gave the Wings a 4-2 lead, and on the overhead screen, they started showing highlights of a Cowboys minicamp. No, I'm kidding. But they might as well have.

BUTT OF JOKES

MANDI WRIGHT

Tomas Holmstrom and Dallas' Steve Ott go at it in the final seconds of the Wings' 3-1 loss in Game 4. Holmstrom was asked what needs to be done in Game 5. "I have to lose some weight," he said. The Wings had a goal called back in Game 4 because referee Kelly Sutherland ruled Holmstrom's posterior violated Marty Turco's airspace.

ROUND 3, GAME 4
STARS 3, WINGS 1

REAR-ENDED

HOLMSTROM'S BACKSIDE CREATED GOAL CONTROVERSY

WINGS LEAD SERIES, 3-1

COUNT 'EM

5

Wins for the Wings' 11th Stanley Cup

BIG STAT

The Stars waited more than 219 minutes for their first lead in this series, and it lasted barely more than a minute, as Henrik Zetterberg tied the game 49 seconds into the third period.

TWO CENTS WORTH
MICHAEL ROSENBERG

The Wings insisted beforehand that they were not looking past Game 4, though they led the series, 3-0. I got the feeling that if I asked Kris Draper if he had a 401(k), he would have said no, because he wasn't thinking past Game 4. He acknowledged that he watched Pittsburgh and Philadelphia in the Eastern Conference finals, but I think he was just doing his part to boost the Versus ratings.

QUOTABLE

"I think it's because referee too much just watch Holmstrom what he do. And if he so much as touch, he just calls it as Holmstrom's fault."

PAVEL DATSYUK, on Holmstrom's reputation with the officials

WINGIN' IT

How one-sided had the series been until Game 4? The Stars didn't even have one of the three stars selected from the first three games. Turco, Brenden Morrow and Mike Modano, the Westland native who scored the game-winner, took the honors this time.

HERO
MARTY TURCO

With his back to the wall, Turco turned in his best effort of the series, stopping 33 shots to give the Stars a glimmer of hope.

GOATS
THE OFFICIALS

They immediately waved off an apparent power-play goal by Pavel Datsyuk in the second period, ruling that Tomas Holmstrom's rear end had interfered with Turco. Loui Eriksson scored a short time later, giving the Stars their first lead of the series.

ROUND 3, GAME 5
STARS 2, WINGS 1

STARBURST
DALLAS' HOPES REVIVED AFTER DETROIT ERRORS

WINGS LEAD SERIES, 3-2

JULIAN H. GONZALEZ

TURCO TAMES WINGS

Ex-Wolverines goalie Marty Turco makes a late game save. His stellar performance led a Ft. Worth columnist to write: "He certainly is a better pure goalie than Osgood. I realize this is not popular in Detroit where a few idiots keep touting him as a Hall of Famer. But last time I checked, standing behind this Red Wings team qualifies you for the Hall of Really Lucky."

TWO CENTS WORTH
MITCH ALBOM

This series is 3-2 now, "on set" as they say in tennis, and anything can happen, and that's a shame for Detroit. Because as stars go, these Stars were fading, flickering to nothing, about to vaporize into a big black hole. Now it's Stars light, Stars bright. Dallas has flickered back, and the red fog over the franchise is lifting. You let a team get up at your own risk. Having had the Stars down, 3-0, it is up to the Wings to finish what they started. Or it's the start of their finish.

QUOTABLE

"When they were in lockdown mode, we didn't get enough people and pucks to the net."

MIKE BABCOCK

COUNT 'EM

5

Wins for the Wings' 11th Stanley Cup

HERO
MARTY TURCO

Finally, the Dallas goalie posted the first Joe Louis Arena victory of his NHL career. It couldn't have come at a better time.

GOAT
CHRIS CHELIOS

He wasn't even on the ice when the winning goal was scored — because his bad line change helped create the space for the play. "I lost sight of the puck," Chelios said. "It was a bad change, and it cost us a goal."

BIG STAT

It had been more than 10 years since Turco's last win at the Joe; he made 18 saves in Michigan's 4-1 win over Lake Superior State that night.

WINGIN' IT

Former NFL quarterback Boomer Esiason was in attendance and had to be beaming with pride when Turco hit Joel Lundqvist up the middle with a Hail Mary pass that led to a breakaway and the game-winner.

ON TO THE FINALS

MANDI WRIGHT

Pavel Datsyuk celebrates with Tomas Holmstrom and Henrik Zetterberg. It would be the first Cup finals for Henrik Zetterberg, who was skating toward royal treatment in Detroit, and who slammed the door closed in Game 6 with the Wings' fourth goal, a short-handed breakaway that left Marty Turco sprawled and helpless.

ROUND 3, GAME 6
WINGS 4, STARS 1

FINALLY!
WINGS ON TRACK, AMBUSH DALLAS

WINGS WIN SERIES, 4-2

COUNT 'EM

4

Wins for the Wings' 11th Stanley Cup

WINGIN' IT
Detroit-Pittsburgh makes it an all-American Stanley Cup finals for the first time since 2003, when New Jersey faced Anaheim.

HERO
DALLAS DRAKE
He assisted on the first goal by shooting a puck off Kris Draper's chin, scored late in the first to make it 3-0, and hit anything and everything all night.

GOAT
BRENDEN MORROW
It was a forgettable night for the Stars captain. He took one shot in 24:03 and was a minus-3.

BIG STAT
Chris Osgood notched his 48th playoff victory, passing Terry Sawchuk for the Wings' all-time lead.

TWO CENTS WORTH
MICHAEL ROSENBERG
The Red Wings face the Pittsburgh Penguins in the Stanley Cup finals, and that is all sorts of perfect. It's the kind of matchup that could send television ratings all the way to the ... uh, top of the basement steps. Hey, that's just reality for hockey right now. When the Wings play the way they did in Game 6, it is hard to imagine anybody beating them. The first period was a true clinic: The Wings got three net-front goals and completely dominated play. When Henrik Zetterberg scored a shorthanded goal in the second period, the Wings had four goals and Dallas had seven shots.

QUOTABLE
"It was a great, strong effort. It's a great feeling being back, going to the finals again, and getting a chance to play for the Cup."
NICKLAS LIDSTROM

ROUND 3, GAME 6
WINGS 4, STARS 1

West, Won

WINGS BRING THE HEAT AND MELT DOWN DALLAS

BY MITCH ALBOM

It was steaming hot outside American Airlines Arena, temperatures in the 90s, bad ice weather, a bad omen for a northern team, and the Red Wings didn't need more bad omens.

But unworthy teams stumble and fall, while worthy champions stumble but come back harder. And so the Wings, after two losses in trying to close the Western Conference finals, came to Texas, stood tall against the fire, then threw themselves into it.

They fronted Stars goalie Marty Turco like a gangster itching for a fight. Kris Draper fronted him until a puck went in off Draper's face. Pavel Datsyuk fronted him and top-shelved a rebound for a goal. Dallas Drake fronted him and chopped until Turco's redwood shield came crashing down, the puck slipped through, and the Stars were snuffed to ashes.

West, won.

On to the Stanley Cup finals.

"Where did that game come from?" someone asked Drake, who had an assist, two blocks and his first goal of the playoffs.

"I sat close to (Henrik) Zetterberg and hoped it would rub off," he said, laughing.

It is the first Cup finals for upcoming talent like Valtteri Filppula, Niklas Kronwall and Jiri Hudler.

And it is a first for an aging, sentimental favorite, 39-year-old Drake, whose last championship came when he was in college. How sweet was the West clincher for him? He assisted on the first goal by Draper with a perfect pass off Draper's face, and he scored the third goal by chopping away at Turco like a man scraping his way out of prison. Drake, old enough to be on his second stint with the Wings, had talked for days about how special this chance was, how he cherished the taste of being this close.

And, oh, yes, the fourth time for a guy named Chris Osgood. Ten years ago, he led the Wings to a title, then was unpro-

SIR DRAKE   MANDI WRIGHT

Dallas Drake, 39, advanced to his first Cup finals by scoring this third-period goal. Drake, whose last championship came when he was in college at Northern Michigan. He assisted on the first goal by Kris Draper with a perfect pass off Draper's face. "I'm not gonna lie, I considered it," Drake said about the possibility of retiring if the Wings lost the series. "It's been 16 years and this is the farthest I've gone and the closest I've come."

tected in the waiver draft. Then he went away, then came back. Then he sat on the bench. And now he has stats that would take the shine off new chrome, and a calm that would put a hypnotist to sleep.

The finals. What a nice ring. Maybe in other cities, six years is nothing. In Hockeytown, it feels like an eternity.

But it's over now. The series. The wait. Trips to Texas. They came to the heat. They saw the heat. They threw themselves in the heat. And there is more hockey to play.

West, won.

CHEERING TOWARD THE CUP FINALS

Jiri Hudler, center, celebrates with Darren Helm and Darren McCarty after Hudler's Game 3 goal. The Wings didn't waste any time in Game 6 after losses in Games 4 and 5. They scored on their first power play. They had three goals in the first 17 minutes. And they advanced to the Cup finals for the first time since winning it in 2002.

JULIAN H. GONZALEZ

ALL GOOD

Chris Osgood was knocked down after being slashed by Dallas' Mike Ribeiro in Game 2. After being outplayed by Marty Turco in a few games, Osgood had a stellar Game 6 and became the Wings' all-time leader with 48 career playoff victories, surpassing Terry Sawchuk. He also returned to the Cup finals for the first time since leading the Wings to the Cup in 1998.

FALLING SHORT

When Henrik Zetterberg scored a shorthanded goal on Marty Turco in the second period, the Wings had four goals and Dallas had seven shots. It was Zetterberg's 11th goal of the playoffs. Detroit was the first Presidents' Trophy winner to make the finals since its 2002 club did it.

MANDI WRIGHT

CHAPTER FIVE

THE FINALS

t is going to get harder. And more fun. Way, way more fun. The Red Wings vs. the Penguins in the Stanley Cup finals.

Fates could not have bestowed upon hockey fans a better finals than the Red Wings against the Penguins.

In the spotlight: three of the league's top-six regular-season scorers: the Wings' Henrik Zetterberg and Pavel Datsyuk, the Penguins' Evgeni Malkin, and a fourth player, Sidney Crosby, who is merely the most important player in the whole league. Anybody who complains about these games probably hates sunshine and picnics.

The finals are back in Hockeytown after a six-year hiatus. Maybe in other cities, six years is nothing. In Hockeytown, it feels like an eternity.

WELCOME TO THE FINALS
The Wings celebrate Mikael Samuelsson's goal in Game 1. Although three-time Stanley Cup winners Steve Yzerman, Brendan Shanahan, Igor Larionov and Sergei Fedorov were gone, the Red Wings still had eight players from their 2002 Cup team — Nicklas Lidstrom, Chris Chelios, Pavel Datsyuk, Kris Draper, Dominik Hasek, Tomas Holmstrom, Kirk Maltby and Darren McCarty.

JULIAN H. GONZALEZ

BETWEEN THE LINES

OCTO MADNESS

AMY LEANG

Red Wings fan Zach Smith, 19, of Cleveland went to Pittsburgh and threw an octopus on the ice at Game 4. He was kicked out, then went back to his car, put on a different shirt and went back into the arena. Jay Roberts, general manager of Mellon Arena, wasn't impressed. "You're not allowed to throw things on the ice in the building, and we kick people out for throwing all sorts of things," he said. "That could have hit somebody."

OPERATION OCTOPUS

BEN SCHMITT

Mike Hartman, left, self-proclaimed head octopus cutter at Wholey's Fish Market in Pittsburgh, helps enforce store owner Dan Wholey's edict: "If you're from Detroit, you're not allowed to buy the octopus. Must show identification."

SIGNS
OF THE TIMES

Pittsburgh Mayor Luke Ravenstahl issued a statement claiming that the winner of the finals would lay claim the "Hockey Town U.S.A." title. Too bad he couldn't spell Hockeytown. It is spelled as one word, not two.

MANDI WRIGHT

YOUTH VS. EXPERIENCE

Red Wings' average age: 32.3; Penguins' average age: 27.9. Detroit had 10 previous Stanley Cup winners, combining for 23 championships on its roster. Pittsburgh had three previous champions and four titles.

TV CONUNDRUM

Detroit fans had issues: What team to watch? The NBA Pistons and NHL Red Wings played at the same time on three days during the Cup finals. There would be no double title, though: The Pistons lost to the Celtics in the Eastern Conference finals.

MAYOR VS. MAYOR

Pittsburgh Mayor Luke Ravenstahl used a chain saw to "clip" the "Red Wings" at a Pittsburgh rally. Detroit Mayor Kwame Kilpatrick and Ravenstahl reached a gentlemen's wager over the series. If Detroit wins, Ravenstahl had to send Kilpatrick goodies from the Steel City, including Heinz Ketchup and Primanti Sandwiches. Get the french fries ready!

BRING YOUR OWN OCTOPI

There was a Pittsburgh fish market with octopi for sale, just not for Detroiters. Dan Wholey, owner of Wholey's Fish Market in Pittsburgh's warehouse section known as the Strip District, said he'd decline the sale of octopus to anyone in Red Wings gear. He said he would also listen for Midwestern accents and maybe check identification.

ABOUT THE PENS

Pittsburgh was in the finals for the first time since 1992, when Mario Lemieux was in his prime. Many considered the Penguins the most exciting team in the league. Much pressure fell on Sid the Kid. If hockey is to return to the American sports consciousness, it needed Sidney Crosby to have a big series.

SCOUTING THE PENGUINS

The Pens had a fearsome top line, headlined by Crosby and Evgeni Malkin. They also had stars Marian Hossa and 19-year-old Jordan Staal. On defense, Sergei Gonchar should have been a finalist for the Norris Trophy. Pittsburgh's Marc-Andre Fleury was second only to Chris Osgood in goals-against average during the playoffs.

TRASH TALK

Gene Collier, of the Pittsburgh Post-Gazette, wrote "Murder City" Detroit was no longer Hockeytown. "Hockeytown just sounds so accomplished and so welcoming. And, you have to admit, it beats the heck out of Murder City. ... That notion reached something of a flashpoint in December, when Sports Illustrated spotlighted some nettlesome facts, such as that of Joe Louis Arena's 20,006 seats, fewer than 15,000 are filled with season-ticket holders."

OF THE STANLEY CUP

AMY LEANG

WELCOME TO PITTSBURGH
Fans who couldn't get into the Game 3 at Mellon Arena watched it outside. It was the first time the Penguins and Red Wings have met in the playoffs, and they had not played in the regular season since Oct. 7, 2006 — a 2-0 Detroit victory in Pittsburgh. The Penguins had not been to the Stanley Cup finals since they won their last championship in 1992.

SAM'S THE MAN

JULIAN H. GONZALEZ

Mikael Samuelsson scores on Marc-Andre Fleury in Game 1. Samuelsson had five shots on goal, more than any Penguins player, second only to teammate Henrik Zetterberg's eight. Samuelsson's final stat line: Two goals, one penalty drawn, five shots, two hits, one takeaway and one blocked shot.

STANLEY CUP FINALS, GAME 1
WINGS 4, PENGUINS 0

SAM SLAM

SAMUELSSON'S GOALS GIVE WINGS TYPE OF EDGE THEY DON'T LOSE

BY MICHAEL ROSENBERG

SAM SHOT   MANDI WRIGHT
The Wings celebrate with Mikael Samuelsson after his second goal of Game 1. He had just two goals in the playoffs entering the game, despite being a second-liner for most of the playoffs and despite being a regular as a right point man on the second power-play unit. His coaches and teammates kept hammering home one thing to him: Shoot the puck, shoot it, shoot it.

Well, that lived up to the preseries hype. And also defied it. These Red Wings-Penguins Stanley Cup finals are supposed to be a hockey fan's dream. And Game 1 certainly was at Joe Louis Arena. But instead of a shoot-out between Pittsburgh's Sidney Crosby and Evgeni Malkin and the Red Wings' Henrik Zetterberg and Pavel Datsyuk, it was a tense, end-to-end, goalie duel.

For most of the night, nobody could score. Except for one guy.

I'm tempted to call Mikael Samuelsson a quiet Swede, but you probably would ask if there is any other kind. Samuelsson normally says so little that he makes teammate and countryman Nicklas Lidstrom seem like Teddy Roosevelt.

But in Game 1, Samuelsson carried the big stick. He scored once in the second and once in the third to give the Wings a 2-0 lead. Dan Cleary and Zetterberg scored late to complete a 4-0 victory, but this was Samuelsson's night.

He scored his first goal when he forced goalie Marc-Andre Fleury to his knees, sped around the back of the net and shoved the puck into the goal. His second goal was not as artistic but just as big. Samuelsson checked defenseman Hal Gill behind the Pittsburgh goal, then broke away and found himself with the puck in front of the net — and nobody between him and Fleury. He took one

whack and scored.

For the first time in years, Detroit seemed like Hockeytown again. Joe Louis Arena was not just sold out. It was full before the opening face-off.

The Wings put faith in their stars; Mike Babcock matched Datsyuk and Zetterberg against Crosby at every chance. Osgood wasn't pressured much, but when he was, he came through.

Pittsburgh should be especially annoyed by Samuelsson's outburst. Five years ago, Samuelsson played for the Penguins — and scored two goals in 22 games. In Game 1, he scored twice in one night.

When Babcock was asked about it afterward, he snapped, "You're setting me up here. You throw me a softball, you want me to respond."

Imagine how he'd feel if the Wings had *lost*.

There was not much chance of that. The Wings were too good.

They preempted the Crosby Show.

"I don't expect it to be easy," Crosby said.

Maybe not. But did he really expect it to be this hard?

PENS RUN DRY

Chris Osgood makes a save on Pittsburgh's Marian Hossa in Game 1. Osgood earned his 12th career postseason shutout and first in the Stanley Cup finals. The Wings outshot the Penguins, 36-19. "We're a different team than what (the Penguins) played before," Osgood said. "We possessed the puck. We like to the majority of the time, if we can. That's the best defense when we have the puck. That's what we believe in. I just think they hadn't seen it before."

STANLEY CUP FINALS, GAME 1
WINGS 4, PENGUINS 0

WINGS LEAD SERIES, 1-0

COUNT 'EM

3

Wins for the Wings' 11th Stanley Cup.

HERO
MIKAEL SAMUELSSON
The former Penguin scored the first two goals — one in the second period and another early in the third — doubling his playoff goal total.

GOAT
MARC-ANDRE FLEURY
The kid goalie faced more shots and looked a little shaky on a couple of goals — especially those two by Mikael Samuelsson.

BIG STAT
7 shots by the Penguins in the second and third periods to 25 by the Red Wings, who finished with a 36-19 edge.

WINGIN' IT
Pittsburgh should be especially annoyed by Samuelsson's outburst. Five years ago, Samuelsson played for the Penguins and scored two goals in 22 games. Now, playing against them in the Stanley Cup finals, he scored twice in one night.

TWO CENTS WORTH
MICHAEL ROSENBERG
I'm tempted to call Mikael Samuelsson a quiet Swede, but you probably would ask if there is any other kind. Samuelsson normally says so little that he makes teammate and countryman Nicklas Lidstrom seem like Teddy Roosevelt.

QUOTABLE

"Sometimes he's got a tendency of pulling up and looking for a pass instead of shooting, but we want him to shoot the puck more."
NICKLAS LIDSTROM,
on Samuelsson.

STANLEY CUP FINALS, GAME 2
WINGS 3, PENGUINS 0

DEFENDERS

STELLAR DEFENSE BACKS GOALS FROM MULTIPLE WINGS

BY MITCH ALBOM

Here came Valtteri Filppula, flying down the ice, beating his defender, who grabbed at him desperately, as if trying to hug a train. Filppula broke free, eye on the puck, dove for it, swinging his stick and — shades of Bobby Orr! — he put that black bullet past the Pittsburgh goalie, then he slid on his belly across the ice. It was fast. It was furious. It was even a bit magical.

"Did you sneak a peek at the replay on the scoreboard?" someone asked Filppula after the 3-0 Game 2 victory at Joe Louis Arena.

"I did, I did," he admitted, smiling sheepishly.

Why not?

Beep, beep. Out of the way. The Red Wings have cruised through two games with barely a blemish. Two shutouts.

For the moment, the guys in the yellow and black seem to be playing Wile E. Coyote in the Road Runner cartoons. Always flattened. Always looking up from the pavement, wondering "What just hit us?" (Or, in Filppula's case, what just flew past?)

Beep. Beep. Was that just Brad Stuart firing a slap shot past Marc-Andre Fleury? Brad Stuart? A defenseman whose biggest playoff production before Game 2 was the birth of his second son?

Beep. Beep. Was that Niklas Kronwall lowering his shoulder and upending Jarkko Ruutu halfway into next week?

Beep, beep. Was that Chris Osgood stopping all 22 shots and upping his playoff legend by getting knocked down in the third period by Ryan Malone, drawing a penalty — and STILL stopping a shot?

Beep, beep. Out of the way.

Which is why I am about to say what I am about to say. Cool it.

Yes, the Wings are doing all they are supposed to do. Yes, they even got Johan Franzen back in Game 2.

Yes, the Wings rendered the Penguins' superstars moot. Sidney Crosby — zero goals. Evgeni Malkin — who not too long ago was being hailed as the best player in the playoffs —

STUART NOT SO LITTLE   JULIAN H. GONZALEZ

Johan Franzen congratulates Brad Stuart after Stuart's first-period goal in Game 2. Stuart had six goals in the regular season and none in 14 games in the playoffs. Trade-day acquisition Stuart couldn't have worked out much better. In addition to being a perfect defensive partner for Niklas Kronwall, he was second on the team in hits in the playoffs.

no shots on goal.

And, yes, the Wings are getting points from their stars as well as the less-likely players.

All good. No argument.

But Pittsburgh has yet to play on its home ice in these finals. And the Penguins have not lost there in more than three months.

And until the Wings snap that, there should be no celebrating, and very little highlight-film watching.

WINGS LEAD SERIES, 2-0

COUNT 'EM

2

Wins for the Wings' 11th Stanley Cup.

HERO
CHRIS OSGOOD
Mr. Zero! After his second straight shutout, Ozzie's one away from tying the Stanley Cup finals record.

GOAT
GARY ROBERTS
What senior leadership? His cheap shot on Johan Franzen led the young Penguins to their frustrated finish.

BIG STAT
The Wings are 19-3 in the regular season and playoffs when Tomas Holmstrom scores.

QUOTABLE

"I guess the way our team's built is we don't have as many North America guys that would be dropping their gloves and fighting right there. We just try to keep our poise and play."

MIKE BABCOCK, on Roberts' cheap shot and the ensuing melee.

TWO CENTS WORTH
DREW SHARP
Johan Franzen returned in Game 2 from his concussion-like symptoms and headaches, getting an assist and giving the Wings another dangerous offensive weapon. That's the equivalent of a Rockefeller winning the lottery. It's Pittsburgh with the headaches now.

WINGIN' IT
Osgood is the first to post shutouts in the first two games of the finals since New Jersey's Martin Brodeur in 2003 against Anaheim.

GARY GOAT
Chris Osgood stops Gary Roberts in Game 2. Roberts enraged Wings fans when he hit the head of Johan Franzen. Franzen had played for the first time since Game 1 of the Dallas series because of concussion-like symptoms.

MANDI WRIGHT

JULIAN H. GONZALEZ

SID THE KID

An airborne Sidney Crosby is all smiles after giving the Penguins their first goal and first lead of the finals in Game 3. "They got to the puck a little quicker at times," Wings coach Mike Babcock said. "They scored first, which helped them. I thought Crosby and (Marian) Hossa were better. More energy and controlled more plays."

KID SHOCK

SIDNEY CROSBY NETS 2 TO GET PENS BACK IN IT

BY DREW SHARP

Finally, there were signs of life in a Cup finals choking from its own unattainable hype. It had become predictable.

The Wings attacked. The Penguins retreated.

The only drama through the first two games was whether Chris Osgood could stay awake long enough to pick up his Conn Smythe Trophy for being the most valuable player of the playoffs. Instead of a mask, he could have worn a nightcap.

The Penguins had one shot on goal through the first 10 minutes of the first period of Game 3.

And then the alarm clock buzzed.

Home was sweet for the Penguins. They found the offensive aggressiveness that deserted them in Detroit, claiming a 3-2 victory.

The Penguins won their 17th straight home game. Their last loss was more than three months ago, explaining the renewed confidence.

So put the brooms away. Forget sweep talk.

The Wings remain in control, but Pittsburgh definitely fired a warning shot.

The Penguins made Osgood work — really work — for the first time in this series. They finally revealed the dynamic offensive personality that carried them through the Eastern Conference playoffs. Young star Sidney Crosby scored the Pens' first two goals, squeezing the first one through Osgood's five-hole after he capitalized on a rare unforced error.

That ended Osgood's shutout streak at 154 minutes, 58 seconds; the previous goal against him came early in the third period at Dallas in Game 6 of the Western Conference finals.

Marian Hossa had two assists. Marc-Andre Fleury stopped 32 shots.

The Wings won't panic. They've never trailed in a series in these playoffs and only once have they been tied — 2-2 in the first round.

The Wings played flawless defensively in the first two games, making Game 3's uncustomary mistakes stand out even more.

It's not often that the team with a 2-1 series lead needs the wake-up call.

DOWNER
Chris Osgood reacts after giving up a third-period goal to ex-Spartan Adam Hall. Wrote Bob Smizik, of the Pittsburgh Post-Gazette: "As well as the Red Wings played in the first two games, recent history tells us they maybe aren't quite that good. They lost twice in their opening-round series against Nashville and twice in the conference final to Dallas."

MANDI WRIGHT

LOSS IN A FLEURY

MANDI WRIGHT

Pavel Datsyuk moves in on Marc-Andre Fleury in Game 3. Fleury looked far more confident. He made 32 saves to Chris Osgood's 21 for the Wings. His win streak at home increased to 19 games.

S T A N L E Y   C U P   F I N A L S ,   G A M E   3
PENGUINS 3, WINGS 2

WINGS LEAD SERIES, 2-1

COUNT 'EM

2

Wins for the Wings' 11th Stanley Cup.

HERO
SIDNEY CROSBY
The Kid finally got the Penguins on the board with a goal late in the first period and another early in the second.

GOAT
BRAD STUART
His loose pass up the middle gave the Pens the puck and the first score, which has been all-important in the playoffs.

BIG STAT
Johan Franzen — who hadn't scored since May 8 — scored his team-record 13th goal, breaking a tie with Henrik Zetterberg.

WINGIN' IT
Former Spartan Adam Hall scored what turned out to be the game-winner in the third period.

TWO CENTS WORTH
BOB SMIZIK, PITTSBURGH POST-GAZETTE
Turns out the Detroit Red Wings might not be a team for the ages. Might not be just about flawless in every phase of the game. Might not be coached by the greatest tactician and motivator in NHL history. It probably came as a surprise to some, particularly those in Michigan, but the Red Wings will not win the Stanley Cup in four games. In fact, they might not win it at all.

QUOTABLE

"They're a team built for playing at home. They feed off the energy of the crowd. This shouldn't come as a big shock. But now, it's on us to respond."

KRIS DRAPER

STANLEY CUP FINALS, GAME 4
WINGS 2, PENGUINS 1

STANLEY CUSP

HUDLER SCORES GAME-WINNING GOAL IN THIRD

BY MITCH ALBOM

The first whistle was bad enough, a penalty in the third period, four men against five. But the second whistle was like a gauntlet smash from the gods.

"You want the Stanley Cup?" it seemed to screech. "Go through this fire and prove it."

So Andreas Lilja skated into the penalty box, joining Kirk Maltby, and the Pittsburgh crowd rose to its feet, and for one minute and 26 seconds the Red Wings would need to protect a one-goal lead with three skaters to the Penguins' five.

What else you got?

The Wings blocked shots. They jammed the passing lanes. Then Henrik Zetterberg stole the puck and took it into the Pittsburgh zone, spinning and weaving and actually firing a shot himself. The seconds ticked. Still no goal.

Maltby out of the box. Lilja out of the box.

Red Wings out of trouble.

What else you got? The Wings took a 3-1 lead in these Stanley Cup finals by defying the shorthanded odds and smashing a three-month curse — the Penguins' perfect record at home. The Wings won Game 4 without their favorite man-in-the-middle, Tomas Holmstrom, who had an injured hamstring. They won despite giving up the first goal.

What else you got?

On the Wings' first goal, Dan Cleary was out there in the Holmstrom spot, out in front of the net, and he created enough distraction to allow a long Nicklas Lidstrom slap shot to go flying past Marc-Andre Fleury. That was huge, because it came less than five minutes after Pittsburgh had scored first, a rare soft goal surrendered by Chris Osgood. The Penguins had not lost in the playoffs when they scored first. But as Osgood later said, "I don't look at streaks and records and who wins when they score first. ... We think we can come back. ... and we knew we could win."

What else you got?

The Wings' star players are playing big (Lidstrom, Zetterberg) and their role players are playing big (Jiri Hudler

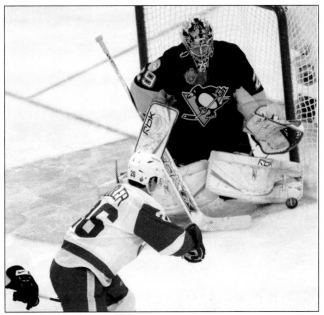

JIRI FEELING   AMY LEANG

Jiri Hudler scored his fifth goal of the playoffs in Game 4, netting the winner with a quick backhand in the third period. "He's a relaxed guy," Franzen said of Hudler. "Nothing seems to get to him. It doesn't matter if somebody tries to hit him, he just steps around them with his quick hands and quick feet, turning and making good plays. He doesn't get that many minutes, but as soon as he gets the puck, he does something with it." Hudler, a fourth-line winger and power-play specialist, starts thinking about shooting as soon as he hits the ice. "That's what Babs wants me to do," he said.

scored the winning goal, after a pass from Brad Stuart and Darren Helm).

They can sniff it now. The aroma of Stanley Cup glory is wafting through the air.

One win to end it all. One win for the throne. What else you got, Pittsburgh? Because the home-ice thing, the first-goal thing, and the five-on-three thing didn't stop the Red Wings.

And it looks like nothing will.

WINGS LEAD SERIES, 3-1

COUNT 'EM

1

Win for the Wings' 11th Stanley Cup.

HERO
CHRIS OSGOOD
Solid as ever in a low-scoring game. Has he clinched the Conn Smythe Trophy yet?

GOAT
EVGENI MALKIN
Half of the Penguins' Big Two of young superstars, he still is pointless in the series. And pretty listless, too.

BIG STAT
The Penguins had won 17 consecutive games at home before the loss. Marc-Andre Fleury had won 19 straight there.

QUOTABLE

"We played great all year long and all through the playoffs. ... Now we're going home to play in the home arena, but we have to play how we want and do the little things right."
HENRIK ZETTERBERG

TWO CENTS WORTH
DREW SHARP
It was a deflating loss for the Penguins, their first at home since Feb. 24. It has been another well-played championship series — plenty of action and excellent scoring chances — something that should excite the NHL. But it's unlikely this series will extend beyond (Game 5).

WINGIN' IT
Zach Smith, 19, of Cleveland was ejected after throwing an octopus on the Mellon Arena ice. But an additional ticket and a change of clothes later got the young Wings fan back into the game to see the ending.

HENRIK TO THE RESCUE
Henrik Zetterberg kicks away a puck delivered by Sidney Crosby during the Penguins' two-man advantage in Game 4. "Oh my God," Dan Cleary said. "We knew the 5-on-3 ... this was it. 'Z' went out there 'Z' was incredible. Single-handedly, he killed almost a minute of time. Proved why he's one of the finest" two-way players in the game."
MANDI WRIGHT

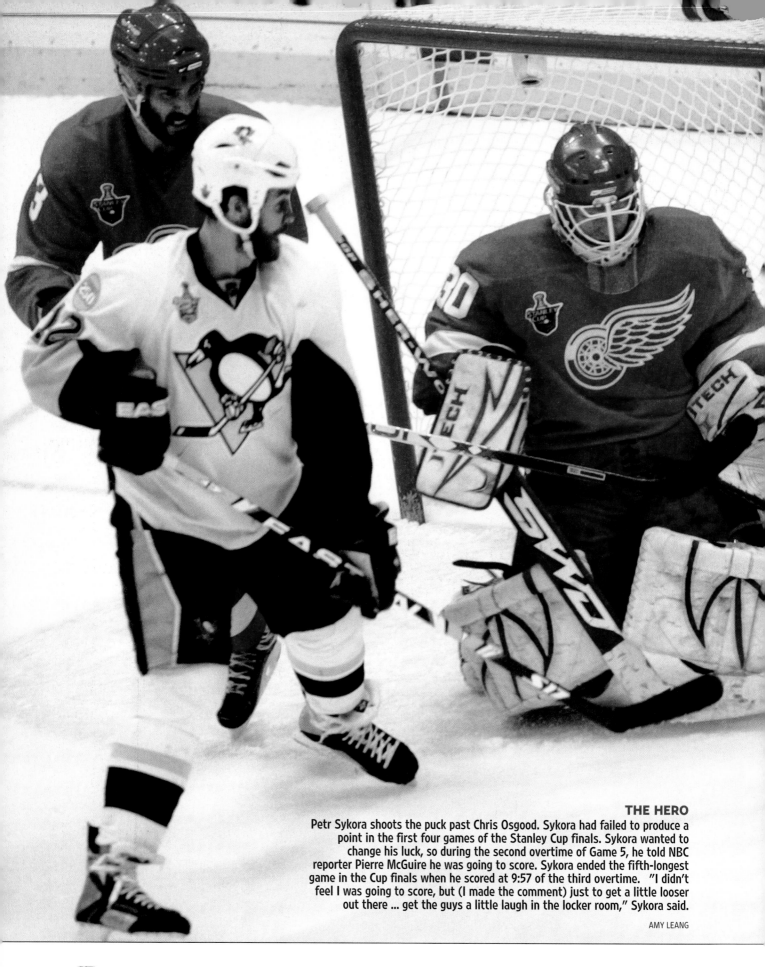

THE HERO

Petr Sykora shoots the puck past Chris Osgood. Sykora had failed to produce a point in the first four games of the Stanley Cup finals. Sykora wanted to change his luck, so during the second overtime of Game 5, he told NBC reporter Pierre McGuire he was going to score. Sykora ended the fifth-longest game in the Cup finals when he scored at 9:57 of the third overtime. "I didn't feel I was going to score, but (I made the comment) just to get a little looser out there ... get the guys a little laugh in the locker room," Sykora said.

AMY LEANG

STANLEY CUP FINALS, GAME 5
PENGUINS 4, WINGS 3 (3 OT)

HELD OVER

35 SECONDS FROM CUP: CELEBRATION TURNS INTO MORATORIUM

BY MITCH ALBOM

AMY LEANG

AND THEY THOUGHT THEY HAD WON
Brian Rafalski is surrounded by Wings after his goal 9:23 into the third period gave Detroit a 3-2 lead. It appeared to be the winner until Maxime Talbot scored with 35 seconds left.

The Red Wings seemed to play an entire season in a single game. They played until the wee hours of the morning, falling behind, scraping to get back, making mistakes, tripping over their own enthusiasm as the mountaintop came into view. They were down two goals. Then they were down one. Then they were tied.

And then, a little less than halfway through the third period, Brian Rafalski, who grew up in Dearborn, whizzed a shot past Marc-Andre Fleury for a 3-2 lead. The Wings were back on top — and you assumed they were staying there. The crowd was on its feet. The Stanley Cup was unloaded. The crowd got louder. The Cup was readied. The crowd was deafening. The Cup was on its way. The city was dreaming about a parade, ready for the biggest hockey party in six years — and then, with the goalie pulled, with 35 seconds left — oh, gosh, it even hurts to write it — Pittsburgh's Maxime Talbot slammed a rebound in past Chris Osgood's left foot, and the crowd, still standing, became 20,000 people who looked as if they'd just witnessed an execution.

And in some ways, they did.

"We felt we had every opportunity to win the game," Mike Babcock would say. But he would say it three overtime periods later. And he would say it after the Cup had been put back in its travel case and the Wings had another plane trip back to Pittsburgh .

Not so fast. What was supposed to be a celebration became a moratorium. One overtime. Two overtimes. And finally, in triple overtime, with players sagging and heaving and fans exhausted and hoarse, finally, the worst came to pass. A four-minute penalty on Jiri Hudler for high-sticking Brooks Orpik. Hudler sat in the penalty box. Orpik was bleeding from the mouth. It was nearly one o'clock in the morning, but you felt the earth move, and you had the feeling, something seismic in the hockey playoffs had just happened.

Moments later, it did. Petr Sykora — one of the few Penguins who has experienced a Stanley Cup — fired a shot from the short side, it went past Osgood.

Red light.

And forget about the coronation. Forget about the five-game series. Forget about the parade you might have envisioned in a couple of days.

The Wings are going back to Pittsburgh . And anything can happen.

FLEURY OF SAVES

Pittsburgh goalie Marc-Andre Fleury makes a kick save on a breakaway attempt by Detroit 's Mikael Samuelsson. Penguins captain Sidney Crosby called Fleury "the savior." "I've known Marc very well, and that's the greatest game he ever played," the Penguins' Maxime Talbot said. "It was probably one of the greatest saves I've seen in the second period against Samuelsson."

STANLEY CUP FINALS, GAME 5
PENGUINS 4, WINGS 3 (3 OT)

WINGS LEAD SERIES, 3-2

COUNT 'EM

1

Wins for the Wings' 11th Stanley Cup.

HERO
MARC-ANDRE FLEURY
The young goalie kept Pittsburgh in the game — stopping 55 shots. Chris Osgood stopped 28 for the Red Wings.

GOAT
JIRI HUDLER
The Wings' fourth-liner's four-minute high-sticking penalty led to Petr Sykora's winning goal 9:57 into the third OT.

BIG STAT
Only four games in Stanley Cup finals history have lasted longer than Game 5's 109 minutes, 57 seconds.

WINGIN' IT
With four minutes left in the second overtime, NBC behind-the-glass reporter Pierre McGuire said Pittsburgh 's Petr Sykora tapped on the glass and said, "I'm going to score."

TWO CENTS WORTH
DREW SHARP
This was Osgood's worst performance of the playoffs. And he knew it, declining to speak with reporters afterward. This performance should silence all the Conn Smythe Award talk. Osgood proved good enough. But they needed greatness (in Game 5).

QUOTABLE

"I hated to see Petr Sykora get that puck late. You just know it's going in. He's that kind of guy. He won a game for me like that in Dallas in five overtimes."
MIKE BABCOCK

RED REIGN

LONG LIVE THE WINGS! STANLEY CUP RETURNS TO HOCKEYTOWN

ROMAIN BLANQUART

THE PUCK STOPS HERE
The puck bounces in front of the Red Wings' goal in the final seconds of Game 6. The Penguins' Marian Hossa had the last scoring chance. "They always have to go right to the bitter end," Detroit goalie Chris Osgood said.

WINGS WIN SERIES, 4-2

COUNT 'EM

0

Win for the Wings' 11th Stanley Cup.

HERO
HENRIK ZETTERBERG
He scored the winning goal and won the Conn Smythe Trophy as playoffs MVP — what more could he do?

GOAT
MARC-ANDRE FLEURY
The Game 5 hero let in a couple of soft goals, including one he pushed in with his rump. That's too much in a tight game.

QUOTABLE

"It's an unbelievable feeling. We've got a great bunch of guys in our dressing room. A lot of people wondered if we could get it done. Once again, our resolve just came through."

KRIS DRAPER

TWO CENTS WORTH
MICHAEL ROSENBERG
Take a moment to salute Ozzie. Nobody can call him a Cup-winning fluke anymore. Take a moment to recognize that he was almost always the solution this spring — and never really the problem.

WINGIN' IT
Ken Kal didn't call the game on radio because he had laryngitis, but he took over for Ken Daniels for the final seconds. "Osgood the save and the rebound. ... Time will run out, and the Detroit Red Wings are the Stanley Cup champion.

NEW CAPTAIN, FAMILIAR CUP

Wings captain Nicklas Lidstrom shows off the Stanley Cup after taking the handoff from NHL commissioner Gary Bettman. Said Bettman: "Nicklas Lidstrom, come get the Stanley Cup. It's yours to take back to Hockeytown." Lidstrom became the first European-born-and-bred player to captain a Stanley Cup champion — and the first Wings captain since Steve Yzerman in 2002.

JULIAN H. GONZALEZ

HOW THE WINGS MADE HISTORY

BY DREW SHARP

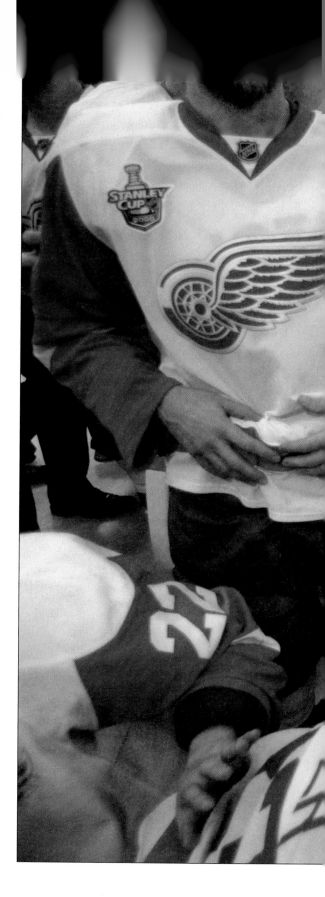

I t's always virtuous exposing a prejudice to the light of common sense. The private whispers that European players couldn't do this or wouldn't do that were worthy of the stable room floor. Such nonsense still existed incrementally within North American hockey cliques, because there was never irrefutable evidence to contradict that myopic thinking. Until Game 6.

The Wings didn't just win a Stanley Cup — they shattered a preconception.

"We never believed all that talk," said Nicklas Lidstrom. "We knew how badly we wanted this and how hard we had to work for it. But it's like anything else. You've got to win to change that kind of thinking."

Normally unemotional, Lidstrom admitted a few tears rolled down his cheeks when commissioner Gary Bettman summoned him to carry out a captain's proudest assignment — receive the Stanley Cup.

This was a historic night — a rewarding night.

The Wings became the first predominantly European team to win the Cup, and the first Cup winner to not have at least one North American-born player among its top-five playoff point producers.

"That finally gets put to rest," said Henrik Zetterberg, the Conn Smythe Trophy winner. "All you heard was how (Europeans) aren't tough enough. It didn't help when we lost early in past playoffs. But this should prove what we already knew about ourselves."

Detroit should take special pride in these champions because ours is a city accustomed to silencing doubters.

As Zetterberg's 13th playoff goal slipped between Pittsburgh goalie Marc-Andre Fleury's legs in the third period, there, too, went the last vestige of a tired, nonsensical fable that European players cared more about winning Olympic gold or world championships than winning the Stanley Cup.

"This is the biggest thing you can do in hockey," said Tomas Holmstrom. "We knew that in Sweden. I'm sure this is going to be a big deal there."

Hockey always will remain Canada's game, but this championship validates that dominance is no longer a birthright.

"I'm very proud being the first European captain to win the Cup," Lidstrom said. "It's great that Hank got the Conn Smythe. It's a great day."

It was a Swede night.

JULIAN H. GONZALEZ

RED, WHITE AND YAHOO!
Darren McCarty (25) helps up goalie Chris Osgood after clinching the Stanley Cup with a 3-2 victory over Pittsburgh in Game 6. McCarty, who scored the Cup-clinching goal for the Wings in 1997, joined the team late in the 2007-08 season. Osgood, the starting goalie for the 1998 Cup champions, went 27-9-4 during the regular season and 14-4 in the playoffs. The Wings celebrated their 11th Cup overall and first since 2002.

STRIKE A POSE
The Red Wings celebrate their fourth Stanley Cup in 11 years. They went 16-6 in the playoffs and were never extended to a seventh game in four series. "I'm so proud of my boys," owner Mike Ilitch said. "They're pretty good hockey players."
JULIAN H. GONZALEZ

HOW SWEDE IT IS!

HANK WINS CONN SMYTHE

BY MICHAEL ROSENBERG

Henrik Zetterberg was supposed to give Sidney Crosby a test. Instead, he gave him a lesson.

Crosby might be the future of the NHL, but Zetterberg was everywhere. Zetterberg won the Conn Smythe Trophy as playoffs MVP, and if you want to figure out why the Red Wings beat the hottest postseason team, start with this:

Zetterberg and Pavel Datsyuk were more complete players than Crosby and Evgeni Malkin.

General manager Ken Holland said of Zetterberg and Datsyuk: "Both of those guys, in my opinion, are the best two-way players in the world."

Datsyuk was great again in Game 6. Zetterberg was greater, down to the final face-off.

"The last face-off, he's out on the ice, and really just taking charge," Kris Draper said. "He kind of came up to me and said, 'You're taking the draw, here's how it's gonna be.' He's a true leader. What he did on both ends of the ice is unbelievable."

This is probably where I should compare Zetterberg to other great Wings forwards. But do you know who he reminds me of? Nicklas Lidstrom. The other Wings always talk about Lidstrom with a sense of wonderment. They say he has no flaws. You can talk about Zetterberg that way now.

"Without a doubt, he brings it every night," Holland said. "He's good in all three zones. The job he did on Sidney Crosby and Malkin, that was a key. And Marian Hossa. Coming into the series we knew we had to do a great job on those guys, and it came down to our top-four defensemen, Pav and Z.

"Z is a special player. He brings it every shift."

Nothing against Crosby and Malkin, but Zetterberg was better. He was more complete. He had six points in six games, but that doesn't tell the story. In every game you could argue that Zetterberg was the best player. Every time he stepped on the ice, he had an impact.

In Game 4, he killed a 5-on-3 power play almost by himself.

In Game 5, he gave the Wings chance after chance to seal the Cup. Even on the Penguins' winning goal, Zetterberg stood out — midway through the third overtime, he was diving to the ice to block a shot.

And I have some bad news for the rest of the NHL: Zetterberg is only 27.

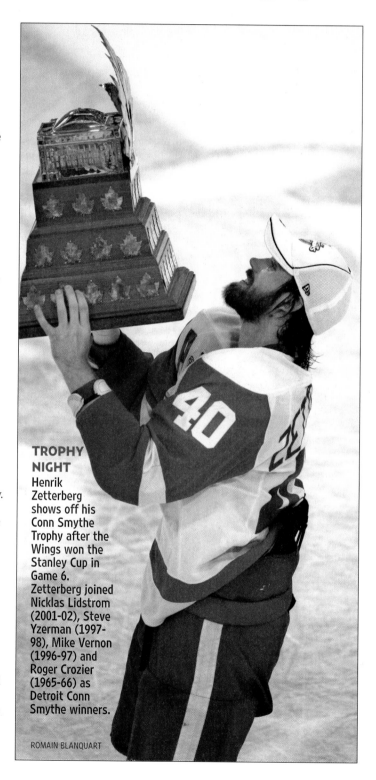

TROPHY NIGHT Henrik Zetterberg shows off his Conn Smythe Trophy after the Wings won the Stanley Cup in Game 6. Zetterberg joined Nicklas Lidstrom (2001-02), Steve Yzerman (1997-98), Mike Vernon (1996-97) and Roger Crozier (1965-66) as Detroit Conn Smythe winners.

ROMAIN BLANQUART

MEMORIES

Highlights of OTHER world events in the 2007-08 season

BY SCOTT BELL

The Red Wings' return to the top of the NHL wasn't the only thing going on around Detroit and the rest of the world during the 2007-08 season. Some other notable events:

BARACK OBAMA and Hillary Clinton fight for the Democratic nomination for president.

DETROIT MAYOR Kwame Kilpatrick fights to keep his job after a text message scandal that cost the city millions.

OTHER CELEBRITIES just plain fight: Rosie-Donald, Britney-K-Fed, Kanye-50 Cent and Lindsay Lohan with — well, everyone.

MICROSOFT OFFERED $44.6 billion to buy Yahoo!

TIGERS GM Dave Dombrowski spends about the same to bring in Miguel Cabrera, Dontrelle Willis, Jacque Jones and Edgar Renteria. All four make the New York Post's 10 worst off-season moves list as the Tigers struggle in the first few months.

AMERICANS GET IN the (involuntary) spending spirit, too, when the average price per gallon of gas reaches $4.

U-M OFFENSIVE TACKLE Jake Long is selected No. 1 overall in the 2008 NFL draft by the Miami Dolphins.

THE NEW ENGLAND PATRIOTS go 18-0 to start the season, only to drop the Super Bowl to the NFC wild card

LLOYD'S LAST RIDE   ERIC SEALS

After losing the opener to Division I-AA Appalachian State, the Wolverines ended the season and Lloyd Carr's tenure on a better note with a 41-35 win over Florida in the Capital One Bowl.

ERIC SEALS

KWAME'S QUANDARY
Detroit Mayor Kwame Kilpatrick fights for his job after a text message scandal revealed he cost the city millions.

New York Giants.

THOSE SAME GIANTS, who Lions QB Jon Kitna said are "not a better football team than us," are just one of the teams that helped the Lions end their '07 season with a 1-7

RASHAUN RUCKER

BOSTON BAKED
The Pistons made a sixth straight Eastern Conference finals, but lost to Kevin Garnett and the Celtics in six games.

mark in their final eight games.

KITNA DOESN'T learn from his past mistake and again says his team should reach 10 wins in 2008.

THE PISTONS make a sixth straight trip to the Eastern

Conference finals ... and a third straight trip to the golf course instead of the NBA Finals after losing to Boston.

U-M COACH Lloyd Carr retires.

THE MICHIGAN unemployment rate hits 6.9% — the highest in the nation.

MICHAEL VICK gets jailed for dogfighting charges; NBA ref Tim Donaghy gets fired for betting on games, and the Mitchell Report exposes performance-enhancing drugs in baseball.

MICHIGAN LOSES its season opener at home, 34-32, to Division I-AA Appalachian State in one of the biggest upsets in history.

WEST VIRGINIA FANS are upset, too. Their coach, Rich Rodriguez, bolts to become Michigan's next coach. He refuses to pay a $4-million buyout, and a lawsuit ensues.

"AMERICAN IDOL" runner-up Chris Daughtry gets a pretty nice consolation prize — his band Daughtry had 2007's best-selling album (3.2 million copies).

DAUGHTRY'S FORMER show keeps its spot atop the ratings, too. "Idol" beats "Dancing With the Stars" for top honors, proving once again that reality doesn't bite.

FOUR SUMMER blockbusters all topped the $300-million box office threshold, but "Spider-Man 3" ($337 million) edged "Shrek the Third" ($323 million) as 2007's best.

BANNER

THE WINGS HAVE 11 TITLES, THOUGH THEY WERE WINLESS FROM 1956-

1936

COACH: Jack Adams (also manager).

HALL OF FAMERS (5): Adams, Marty Barry, Ebbie Goodfellow, Syd Howe, Herbie Lewis.

LEADING SCORER: Barry, 48 games, 21-19-40 in regular season.

GOALIE: Normie Smith, 48 games, 24 wins, 6 shutouts, 2.04 goals-against average.

THE FINALS: Detroit beat Toronto, 3-1.

NOTABLE: Pete Kelly scored the Cup-clinching goal in a 3-2 victory.

1937

COACH: Jack Adams.

HALL OF FAMERS (5): Adams, Marty Barry, Ebbie Goodfellow, Syd Howe, Herbie Lewis.

LEADING SCORER: Barry, 48 games, 17-27-44.

GOALIE: Normie Smith, 48 games, 25 wins, 6 SO, 2.05 GAA.

THE FINALS: Detroit beat N.Y. Rangers, 3-2.

NOTABLE: Wings became the first U.S. team to repeat as champions.

1943

COACH: Ebbie Goodfellow (player/coach).

HALL OF FAMERS (6): Sid Abel, Jack Adams (manager), Goodfellow, Syd Howe, Jack Stewart, Harry Watson.

LEADING SCORER: Howe, 50 games, 20-35-55.

GOALIE: Johnny Mowers, 50 games, 25 wins, 6 SO, 2.47 GAA, Vezina Trophy.

THE FINALS: Detroit beat Boston, 4-0.

NOTABLE: Mowers blanked the Bruins in the final two games, and Joe Carveth scored the Cup winner.

1950

COACH: Tommy Ivan.

HALL OF FAMERS (9): Sid Abel, Jack Adams (manager), Gordie Howe, Ivan, Red Kelly, Ted Lindsay, Harry Lumley, Marcel Pronovost, Jack Stewart.

LEADING SCORER: Lindsay, 69 games, 23-55-78, Art Ross Trophy.

GOALIE: Lumley, 63 games, 33 wins, 7 SO, 2.35 GAA.

THE FINALS: Detroit beat Toronto, 4-3.

NOTABLE: The Production Line — Abel (2), Lindsay (1) and Howe (3) — had the league's top scorers. Howe suffered a near-fatal head injury in Game 1 against Toronto and missed the rest of the series.

1952

COACH: Tommy Ivan.

HALL OF FAMERS (9): Sid Abel, Jack Adams (manager), Alex Delvecchio, Gordie Howe, Ivan, Red Kelly, Ted Lindsay, Marcel Pronovost, Terry Sawchuk.

LEADING SCORER: Howe, 70 games, 47-39-86, Art Ross Trophy, Hart Trophy.

GOALIE: Sawchuk, 70 games, 44 wins, 12 SO, 1.90 GAA, Vezina Trophy.

THE FINALS: Detroit beat Montreal, 4-0.

NOTABLE: The Montreal series marked the introduction of octopi to the Olympia ice.

YEARS

1996, THE LONGEST DROUGHT IN THE LEAGUE. THE OTHER TITLES:

1954

COACH: Tommy Ivan.

HALL OF FAMERS (9): Jack Adams (manager), Al Arbour, Alex Delvecchio, Gordie Howe, Ivan, Red Kelly, Ted Lindsay, Marcel Pronovost, Terry Sawchuk.

LEADING SCORER: Howe, 70 games, 33-48-81, Art Ross Trophy

GOALIE: Sawchuk, 67 games, 35 wins, 12 SO, 1.93 GAA.

THE FINALS: Detroit beat Montreal, 4-3.

NOTABLE: A goal at 4:29 in OT by Tony Leswick gave Detroit the title in a 2-1 victory.

*CONN SMYTHE TROPHY FIRST AWARDED IN 1964-65.

1955

COACH: Jimmy Skinner.

HALL OF FAMERS (7): Jack Adams (manager), Alex Delvecchio, Gordie Howe, Red Kelly, Ted Lindsay, Marcel Pronovost, Terry Sawchuk.

LEADING SCORER: Earl (Dutch) Reibel, 70 games, 25-41-66.

GOALIE: Sawchuk, 68 games, 40 wins, 12 SO, 1.96 GAA, Vezina Trophy.

THE FINALS: Detroit beat Montreal, 4-3.

NOTABLE: Montreal was missing suspended star Maurice (Rocket) Richard. Howe scored the Cup-winning goal.

1997

COACH: Scotty Bowman.

HALL OF FAMERS (2): Bowman, Slava Fetisov.

TOP PLAYERS: Sergei Fedorov, Vladimir Konstantinov, Nicklas Lidstrom, Brendan Shanahan, Steve Yzerman.

LEADING SCORER: Shanahan, 81 games (two with Hartford), 47-41-88.

GOALIES: Chris Osgood, 47 games, 23 wins, 6 SO, 2.30 GAA. Mike Vernon, 33 games, 13 wins, 2.43 GAA.

THE FINALS: Detroit beat Philadelphia, 4-0.

CONN SMYTHE: Vernon.

NOTABLE: The Wings wore down opponents with four lines, stellar defense and solid goaltending.

1998

COACH: Scotty Bowman.

HALL OF FAMERS (2): Bowman, Slava Fetisov

TOP PLAYERS: Sergei Fedorov, Slava Kozlov, Igor Larionov, Nicklas Lidstrom, Larry Murphy, Brendan Shanahan, Steve Yzerman.

LEADING SCORER: Yzerman, 75 games, 24-45-69.

GOALIE: Chris Osgood, 64 games, 33 wins, 6 SO, 2.21 GAA.

THE FINALS: Detroit beat Washington, 4-0.

CONN SMYTHE: Yzerman.

NOTABLE: The Wings dedicated the Cup defense to Konstantinov, whose career ended in a limousine accident after a post-Cup team outing.

2002

COACH: Scotty Bowman.

HALL OF FAMER (1): Bowman.

TOP PLAYERS: Chris Chelios, Sergei Fedorov, Brett Hull, Igor Larionov, Nicklas Lidstrom, Luc Robitaille, Brendan Shanahan, Steve Yzerman.

LEADING SCORER: Shanahan, 80 games, 37-38-75.

GOALIE: Dominik Hasek, 65 games, 41 wins, 5 SO, 2.17 GAA.

THE FINALS: Detroit beat Carolina, 4-1.

CONN SMYTHE: Lidstrom.

NOTABLE: A roster full of future Hall of Famers, including newcomers Hasek, Hull and Robitaille.

REGULAR-SEASON SCHEDULE/RESULTS

OCTOBER

	OPPONENT	RESULT	W-L-OL	GOALIE	TOP PERFORMER	SF-SA	PP	PK
Oct 3	Anaheim	W 3-2 (SO)	1-0-0	D. Hasek	H. Zetterberg, G: 1, A: 1	42-15	2-7	4-5
Oct 6	@ Chicago	L 3-4 (SO)	1-0-1	D. Hasek	N. Lidstrom, G: 1, A: 1	26-27	2-7	4-4
Oct 8	Edmonton	W 4-2	2-0-1	D. Hasek	M. Samuelsson, G: 1, A: 1	35-20	1-5	4-4
Oct 10	Calgary	W 4-2	3-0-1	C. Osgood	P. Datsyuk, G: 0, A: 2	28-21	2-3	2-2
Oct 12	Chicago	L 2-3	3-1-1	D. Hasek	H. Zetterberg, G: 1, A: 0	36-29	0-5	6-8
Oct 14	@ LA Kings	W 4-1	4-1-1	C. Osgood	P. Datsyuk, G: 1, A: 2	30-28	0-2	5-6
Oct 15	@ Anaheim	L 3-6	4-2-1	D. Hasek	H. Zetterberg, G: 1, A: 0	35-29	1-9	9-11
Oct 18	@ San Jose	W 4-2	5-2-1	D. Hasek	B. Rafalski, G: 0, A: 3	27-25	2-5	4-5
Oct 20	@ Phoenix	W 5-2	6-2-1	D. Hasek	K. Maltby, G: 2, A: 0	42-21	0-3	6-6
Oct 24	Vancouver	W 3-2	7-2-1	D. Hasek	T. Holmstrom, G: 2, A: 0	39-15	1-4	4-5
Oct 26	San Jose	W 5-1	8-2-1	D. Hasek	H. Zetterberg, G: 1, A: 0	39-11	0-6	1-2
Oct 28	@ Vancouver	W 3-2	9-2-1	C. Osgood	C. Osgood, SV%: 0.93	32-29	0-2	5-5
Oct 30	@ Edmonton	W 2-1	10-2-1	C. Osgood	C. Osgood, SV%: 0.94	34-16	1-3	3-3

NOVEMBER

	OPPONENT	RESULT	W-L-OL	GOALIE	TOP PERFORMER	SF-SA	PP	PK
Nov 1	@ Calgary	W 4-1	11-2-1	C. Osgood	C. Osgood,SV%: 0.96	26-27	2-3	7-7
Nov 7	Nashville	W 3-2 (SO)	12-2-1	C. Osgood	C. Osgood, SV%: 0.93	45-30	2-8	5-5
Nov 9	Columbus	W 4-1	13-2-1	D. Hasek	D. Cleary, G: 2, A: 0	36-16	2-6	6-7
Nov 11	@ Chicago	L 2-3	13-3-1	C. Osgood	J. Hudler, G: 1, A: 1	32-27	0-6	4-6
Nov 13	@ St. Louis	L 3-4	13-4-1	D. Hasek	N. Kronwall, G: 0, A: 2	30-16	0-4	3-5
Nov 17	Chicago	L 3-5	13-5-1	D. Hasek	H. Zetterberg, G: 1, A: 1	42-17	1-5	3-3
Nov 18	@ Columbus	W 5-4 (SO)	14-5-1	C. Osgood	N. Lidstrom, G: 1, A: 2	35-40	2-4	2-5
Nov 21	St. Louis	W 3-0	15-5-1	C. Osgood	D. Cleary, G: 1, A: 1	38-12	2-11	3-3
Nov 22	@ Nashville	L 2-3	15-6-1	C. Osgood	H. Zetterberg, G: 1, A: 0	30-29	2-8	6-7
Nov 24	@ Columbus	L 2-3 (SO)	15-6-2	C. Osgood	P. Datsyuk, G: 1, A: 1	25-28	1-3	4-4
Nov 27	Calgary	W 5-3	16-6-2	C. Osgood	P. Datsyuk, G: 2, A: 1	35-22	1-7	4-5
Nov 29	Tampa Bay	W 4-2	17-6-2	C. Osgood	D. Cleary, G: 1, A: 0	39-23	1-2	3-3

DECEMBER

	OPPONENT	RESULT	W-L-OL	GOALIE	TOP PERFORMER	SF-SA	PP	PK
Dec 1	Phoenix	W 3-2	18-6-2	C. Osgood	H. Zetterberg, G: 1, A: 1	39-26	2-4	3-3
Dec 4	@ Montreal	W 4-1	19-6-2	D. Hasek	P. Datsyuk, G: 2, A: 1	34-16	1-3	5-5
Dec 7	Minnesota	W 5-0	20-6-2	D. Hasek	H. Zetterberg, G: 3, A: 0	34-19	1-2	4-4
Dec 9	Carolina	W 5-2	21-6-2	D. Hasek	J. Hudler, G: 0, A: 3	38-17	1-7	4-5
Dec 10	@ Nashville	W 2-1	22-6-2	C. Osgood	C. Osgood, SV%: 0.97	35-31	0-6	7-7
Dec 13	Edmonton	L 3-4 (SO)	22-6-3	D. Hasek	H. Zetterberg, G: 2, A: 0	42-25	1-4	3-4
Dec 15	Florida	W 5-2	23-6-3	C. Osgood	C. Osgood, SV%: 0.94	46-35	3-6	3-3
Dec 17	Washington	W 4-3 (SO)	24-6-3	D. Hasek	H. Zetterberg, G: 2, A: 1	30-30	2-4	5-7
Dec 19	LA Kings	W 6-2	25-6-3	D. Hasek	N. Kronwall, G: 0, A: 4	35-20	2-5	3-4
Dec 20	@ St. Louis	L 2-3	25-7-3	C. Osgood	N. Lidstrom, G: 0, A: 1	36-24	0-4	2-4
Dec 22	@ Minnesota	W 4-1	26-7-3	D. Hasek	D. Cleary, G: 1, A: 0	51-19	1-7	1-2
Dec 26	@ St. Louis	W 5-0	27-7-3	C. Osgood	C. Osgood, SV%: 1.00	27-20	2-3	5-5
Dec 27	@ Colorado	W 4-2	28-7-3	C. Osgood	V. Filppula, G: 2, A: 0	29-24	0-1	4-4
Dec 29	@ Phoenix	W 4-2	29-7-3	C. Osgood	P. Datsyuk, G: 1, A: 2	35-34	1-3	4-4
Dec 31	St. Louis	L 0-2	29-8-3	D. Hasek	D. Hasek, SV%: 0.96	31-23	0-4	5-5

JANUARY

	OPPONENT	RESULT	W-L-OL	GOALIE	TOP PERFORMER	SF-SA	PP	PK
Jan 2	Dallas	W 4-1	30-8-3	C. Osgood	C. Osgood, SV%: 0.96	26-24	0-3	3-3
Jan 5	@ Dallas	W 3-0	31-8-3	D. Hasek	D. Hasek, SV%: 1.00	23-22	0-2	2-2
Jan 6	@ Chicago	W 3-1	32-8-3	C. Osgood	C. Osgood, SV%: 0.95	28-20	1-2	2-2
Jan 8	Colorado	W 1-0	33-8-3	D. Hasek	D. Hasek, SV%: 1.00	25-19	0-2	1-1
Jan 10	Minnesota	L 5-6 (SO)	33-8-4	C. Osgood	D. Cleary, G: 1, A: 2	46-28	0-5	4-4
Jan 12	@ Ottawa	L 2-3	33-9-4	D. Hasek	H. Zetterberg, G: 0, A: 1	29-32	1-6	3-5
Jan 15	Atlanta	L 1-5	33-10-4	C. Osgood	M. Samuelsson, G: 0, A: 1	47-25	0-2	1-4
Jan 17	Vancouver	W 3-2 (SO)	34-10-4	D. Hasek	D. Cleary, G: 0, A: 2	49-28	0-3	2-2
Jan 19	@ San Jose	W 6-3	35-10-4	D. Hasek	N. Lidstrom, G: 1, A: 2	28-18	2-5	3-6
Jan 22	@ LA Kings	W 3-0	36-10-4	C. Osgood	C. Osgood, SV%: 1.00	27-27	0-3	2-2
Jan 23	@ Anaheim	W 2-1	37-10-4	D. Hasek	D. Hasek, SV%: 0.96	33-25	1-6	4-5
Jan 30	Phoenix	W 3-2	38-10-4	C. Osgood	N. Lidstrom, G: 1, A: 2	39-34	0-3	1-1

FEBRUARY

	OPPONENT	RESULT	W-L-OL	GOALIE	TOP PERFORMER	SF-SA	PP	PK
Feb 1	Colorado	W 2-0	39-10-4	D. Hasek	P. Datsyuk, G: 0, A: 2	36-15	0-4	3-3
Feb 2	@ Colorado	W 4-0	40-10-4	C. Osgood	P. Datsyuk, G: 1, A: 1	32-23	1-4	4-4
Feb 5	@ Minnesota	W 3-2 (OT)	41-10-4	D. Hasek	D. Cleary, G: 1, A: 1	38-26	0-3	3-4
Feb 7	LA Kings	L 3-5	41-11-4	C. Osgood	H. Zetterberg, G: 2, A: 0	29-25	0-3	3-5
Feb 9	@ Toronto	L 2-3 (OT)	41-11-5	D. Hasek	N. Lidstrom, G: 2, A: 1	34-25	0-2	1-2
Feb 10	Anaheim	L 2-3	41-12-5	C. Osgood	N. Lidstrom, G: 0, A: 1	29-19	2-8	2-2
Feb 12	@ Nashville	L 2-4	41-13-5	C. Osgood	J. Howard, SV%: 0.95	42-23	2-6	5-5
Feb 15	Columbus	L 1-5	41-14-5	C. Osgood	P. Datsyuk, G: 1, A: 0	21-23	1-4	3-5
Feb 17	@ Dallas	L 0-1	41-15-5	J. Howard	J. Howard, SV%: 0.97	28-31	0-4	4-4
Feb 18	@ Colorado	W 4-0	42-15-5	C. Osgood	P. Datsyuk, G: 0, A: 3	40-18	2-6	3-3
Feb 22	@ Calgary	L 0-1	42-16-5	C. Osgood	C. Osgood, SV%: 0.96	38-26	0-6	5-5
Feb 23	@ Vancouver	L 1-4	42-17-5	J. Howard	D. Meech, G: 0, A: 1	29-35	1-7	3-5
Feb 26	@ Edmonton	L 3-4 (SO)	42-17-6	C. Osgood	M. Samuelsson, G: 0, A: 1	43-29	2-7	5-6
Feb 29	San Jose	L 2-3	42-18-6	D. Hasek	H. Zetterberg, G: 1, A: 1	22-22	2-4	2-3

MARCH

	OPPONENT	RESULT	W-L-OL	GOALIE	TOP PERFORMER	SF-SA	PP	PK
Mar 2	@ Buffalo	W 4-2	43-18-6	D. Hasek	J. Franzen, G: 1, A: 1	39-24	1-5	4-5
Mar 5	St. Louis	W 4-1	44-18-6	D. Hasek	P. Datsyuk, G: 2, A: 0	32-19	0-6	3-4
Mar 9	Nashville	W 4-3	45-18-6	D. Hasek	J. Franzen, G: 2, A: 0	33-23	3-8	5-7
Mar 11	Chicago	W 3-1	46-18-6	C. Osgood	P. Datsyuk, G: 1, A: 0	47-20	0-2	2-2
Mar 13	Dallas	W 5-3	47-18-6	C. Osgood	P. Datsyuk, G: 2, A: 1	31-19	1-6	1-2
Mar 15	Nashville	L 1-3	47-19-6	C. Osgood	C. Osgood, SV%: 0.92	35-27	0-6	3-3
Mar 16	@ Columbus	L 3-4	47-20-6	D. Hasek	J. Franzen, G: 2, A: 0	46-17	2-6	2-2
Mar 19	Columbus	W 3-1	48-20-6	D. Hasek	H. Zetterberg, G: 3, A: 0	27-23	1-5	6-7
Mar 20	@ Nashville	W 6-3	49-20-6	D. Hasek	P. Datsyuk, G: 2, A: 0	36-29	1-6	4-5
Mar 22	@ Columbus	W 4-1	50-20-6	D. Hasek	P. Datsyuk, G: 1, A: 2	21-12	2-5	5-5
Mar 25	@ St. Louis	W 2-1	51-20-6	C. Osgood	C. Osgood, SV%: 0.94	32-18	1-5	3-3
Mar 28	St. Louis	L 3-4 (OT)	51-20-7	C. Osgood	H. Zetterberg, G: 0, A: 3	39-21	2-7	5-6
Mar 30	Nashville	W 1-0 (OT)	52-20-7	D. Hasek	D. Hasek, SV%: 1.00	36-22	0-5	6-6

APRIL

	OPPONENT	RESULT	W-L-OL	GOALIE	TOP PERFORMER	SF-SA	PP	PK
Apr 2	@ Chicago	L 2-6	52-21-7	D. Hasek	K. Maltby, G: 1, A: 0	28-28	1-6	6-8
Apr 3	Columbus	W 3-2	53-21-7	D. Hasek	P. Datsyuk, G: 0, A: 2	39-22	1-7	5-6
Apr 6	Chicago	W 4-1	54-21-7	D. Hasek	D. Hasek, SV%: 0.96	38-28	2-5	3-4

PLAYOFFS

FIRST-ROUND SCHEDULE/RESULTS

APRIL

	OPPONENT	RESULT	W-L-OL	GOALIE	TOP PERFORMER	SF-SA	PP	PK
Apr 10	Nashville	W 3-1	1-0-0	D. Hasek	H. Zetterberg, G: 2, A: 0	40-20	0-4	4-4
Apr 12	Nashville	W 4-2	2-0-0	D. Hasek	B. Rafalski, G: 0, A: 2	38-27	1-6	4-5
Apr 14	@ Nashville	L 3-5	2-1-0	D. Hasek	J. Hudler, G: 1, A: 1	26-29	1-4	3-3
Apr 16	@ Nashville	L 2-3	2-2-0	D. Hasek	P. Datsyuk, G: 2, A: 0	41-27	1-5	4-5
Apr 18	Nashville	W 2-1 (OT)	3-2-0	C. Osgood	J. Franzen, G: 1, A: 1	54-21	0-3	3-3
Apr 20	@ Nashville	W 3-0	4-2-0	C. Osgood	C. Osgood, SV%: 1.00	43-20	0-4	3-3

CONFERENCE SEMIFINALS SCHEDULE/RESULTS

APRIL

	OPPONENT	RESULT	W-L-OL	GOALIE	TOP PERFORMER	SF-SA	PP P K
Apr 24	Colorado	W 4-3	5-2-0	C. Osgood	J. Franzen, G: 2, A: 1	36-21	1-5 3-3
Apr 26	Colorado	W 5-4	6-2-0	C. Osgood	J. Franzen, G: 3, A: 0	40-20	2-7 5-5
Apr 29	@ Colorado	W 4-3	7-2-0	C. Osgood	P. Datsyuk, G: 2, A: 1	35-33	2-7 3-5

MAY

	OPPONENT	RESULT	W-L-OL	GOALIE	TOP PERFORMER	SF-SA	PP	PK
May 1	@ Colorado	W 8-2	8-2-0	C. Osgood	H. Zetterberg, G: 2, A: 2	40-31	2-4	3-5

CONFERENCE FINALS SCHEDULE/RESULTS

MAY

	OPPONENT	RESULT	W-L-OL	GOALIE	TOP PERFORMER	SF-SA	PP	PK
May 8	Dallas	W 4-1	9-2-0	C. Osgood	C. Osgood, SV%: 0.95	31-21	3-7	4-4
May 10	Dallas	W 2-1	10-2-0	C. Osgood	H. Zetterberg, G: 1, A: 0	34-18	1-6	4-5
May 12	@ Dallas	W 5-2	11-2-0	C. Osgood	P. Datsyuk, G: 3, A: 0	21-18	0-3	6-6
May 14	@ Dallas	L 1-3	11-3-0	C. Osgood	H. Zetterberg, G: 1, A: 0	34-22	0-6	3-4
May 17	Dallas	L 1-2	11-4-0	C. Osgood	P. Datsyuk, G: 0, A: 1	39-21	1-3	4-4
May 19	@ Dallas	W 4-1	12-4-0	C. Osgood	C. Osgood, SV%: 0.97	29-29	1-2	6-7

STANLEY CUP FINALS SCHEDULE/RESULTS

MAY/JUNE

	OPPONENT	RESULT	W-L-OL	GOALIE	TOP PERFORMER	SF-SA	PP	PK
May 24	Pittsburgh	W 4-0	13-4-0	C. Osgood	C. Osgood, SV%: 1.00	36-19	1-6	5-5
May 26	Pittsburgh	W 3-0	14-4-0	C. Osgood	C. Osgood, SV%: 1.00	34-22	0-8	3-3
May 28	@ Pittsburgh	L 2-3	14-5-0	C. Osgood	J. Franzen, G: 1, A: 0	34-24	1-5	2-3
May 31	@ Pittsburgh	W 2-1	15-5-0	C. Osgood	C. Osgood, SV%: 0.96	30-23	0-3	5-6
June 2	Pittsburgh	L 4-3 (3OT)	15-6-0	C. Osgood	B. Rafalski, G: 1, A: 1	58-32	1-5	4-5
June 4	@Pittsburgh	W 3-2	16-6-0	C. Osgood	H. Zetterberg, G:1, A: 1	30-22	1-3	3-5